In this intriguing narrative in political theory, Booth and Baert trace the multi-layered and often surprising connections between the conservative philosophy of the Nazi jurist Carl Schmitt and the progressive populism of Podemos. In the process they consider the analogies between Weimar Germany and contemporary Spain, General Franco's regime and the warm reception for Schmitt's views on power, the political, the "exception", and decisionism. In tracing the connections between the Podemos leadership and Schmitt's critique of liberalism and parliamentary democracy, they also describe the profound crisis within the European Union between Germany and its underdeveloped periphery. A tour de force, the authors develop a compelling historical sociology of ideas and expose the ambiguities of populism as appealing to extreme right and left politics, and simultaneously dissolving this political division.

Bryan S. Turner ACU (Melbourne) and Potsdam University Germany

The Dark Side of Podemos?

In 2014 a new progressive party, Podemos, emerged on the Spanish political scene. Within just over two years it had become the country's third biggest party, winning a slew of seats in parliament and regularly making headline news. While some saw Podemos as the saviour of Spanish democracy, others accused it of corrosive populism. But what few noticed was that behind its distinctive rhetoric lay a thinker closely associated with Germany's Third Reich: Carl Schmitt.

Why did an ostensibly progressive and avowedly anti-fascist political party take up Schmitt's ideas? The puzzle only deepens when we learn of Schmitt's links with Francisco Franco's dictatorship. In *The Dark Side of Podemos?*, Booth and Baert explain why Schmittian theory resonated with Podemos' founders. In doing so, the authors position Podemos and the ideas that guide it within the context of recent Spanish history and ongoing politics of memory, revealing a story about how personal and political narratives have combined to produce a formidable political force.

This enlightening monograph will appeal to undergraduates and postgraduates, as well as postdoctoral researchers, interested in fields such as Politics, Political Theory and Sociology. It will also be relevant to those curious about contemporary Spanish politics, the nature of populism, the future of the European left, or Carl Schmitt and his links with Spain.

Josh Booth is a Teaching Associate in the Department of Sociology at the University of Cambridge, UK.

Patrick Baert is Professor of Social Theory at the University of Cambridge, UK.

Routledge Advances in Sociology

For a full list of titles in this series, please visit www.routledge.com/series/ SE0511

Social Generativity
A Relational Paradigm for Social Change
Edited by Mauro Magatti

The Live Art of Sociology
Cath Lambert

Video Games as Culture
Considering the Role and Importance of Video Games in Contemporary Society
Daniel Muriel and Garry Crawford

The Sociology of Central Asian Youth
Choice, Constraint, Risk
Mohd. Aslam Bhat

Indigenous Knowledge Production
Navigating Humanity within a Western World
Marcus Woolombi Waters

Time and Temporality in Transitional and Post-Conflict Societies
Edited by Natascha Mueller-Hirth and Sandra Rios Oyola

Practicing Art/Science
Experiments in an Emerging Field
Edited by Philippe Sormani, Guelfo Carbone and Priska Gisler

The Dark Side of Podemos?
Carl Schmitt and Contemporary Progressive Populism
Josh Booth and Patrick Baert

Intergenerational Family Relations
An Evolutionary Social Science Approach
Antti O. Tanskanen and Mirkka Danielsbacka

The Dark Side of Podemos?
Carl Schmitt and Contemporary Progressive Populism

Josh Booth and Patrick Baert

LONDON AND NEW YORK

First published 2018
by Routledge
2 Park Square, Milton Park, Abingdon, Oxon OX14 4RN

and by Routledge
711 Third Avenue, New York, NY 10017

Routledge is an imprint of the Taylor & Francis Group, an informa business

© 2018 Josh Booth and Patrick Baert

The right of Josh Booth and Patrick Baert to be identified as authors of this work has been asserted by them in accordance with sections 77 and 78 of the Copyright, Designs and Patents Act 1988.

All rights reserved. No part of this book may be reprinted or reproduced or utilised in any form or by any electronic, mechanical, or other means, now known or hereafter invented, including photocopying and recording, or in any information storage or retrieval system, without permission in writing from the publishers.

Trademark notice: Product or corporate names may be trademarks or registered trademarks, and are used only for identification and explanation without intent to infringe.

British Library Cataloguing in Publication Data
A catalogue record for this book is available from the British Library

Library of Congress Cataloging in Publication Data
A catalog record for this book has been requested

ISBN: 978-0-8153-8072-6 (hbk)
ISBN: 9781351212557 (ebk)

Typeset in Galliard
by Taylor & Francis Books

Contents

	Acknowledgements	viii
1	The Schmitt-Podemos connection	1
2	Podemos' encounter with Schmitt	20
3	Divergent presents	44
4	Imagining the political past	65
5	Imagining the political future	101
6	Tensions within	117
	Index	128

Acknowledgements

We would like to thank Emily Briggs and Elena Chiu from Routledge who have provided continuous support for this project. We are immensely grateful to Tiago Carvalho, Duncan Kelly, Jeff Miley and Peter Wagner; each took time to cast an expert eye on this manuscript, providing useful feedback. Vera Chapman Browne's copy-editing was excellent and so was Marina Hambach's additional editorial assistance. The comments by the anonymous readers were extremely valuable. Thanks too to Alex Lau-Zhu, without whose support the book would not have been possible.

The research leading to these results has received funding from the European Union Seventh Framework Programme (FP7/2007–2013) under Grant Agreement no. 319974 (INTERCO-SSH). Some of our findings were presented at the final conference of the INTERCO-SSH project at the École des hautes études en sciences sociales (EHESS) in Paris (23–25 February 2017), and the discussions at the conference were very helpful. In the context of this research project, we benefited from conversations with Christian Fleck, Johan Heilbron, Victor Karady, Marco Santoro, Gisèle Sapiro and Gustavo Sorà.

1 The Schmitt-Podemos connection

In 1977, almost two years after the death of Francisco Franco, the German jurist Carl Schmitt published an article in the Spanish newspaper *El País* calling for an amnesty, "a mutual act of forgetting" (Schmitt, 1977). "An amnesty in the true and authentic sense of the word", Schmitt wrote, "signifies nothing less than the end of civil war". By this time almost forty years had passed since the end of the Spanish Civil War (1936–39), and just over thirty years since the defeat of German National Socialism, the political movement with which Schmitt is most closely associated. Since 1945 Schmitt had been unable to work in German academia because he had refused to accept his own denazification, expecting, perhaps, that he himself would be granted the dignity of amnesty. But in Spain he had found something of a second home. It was through his daughter Anima—married from the 1960s to Alfonso Otero, a Spanish professor of legal history, and living in Spain—that Schmitt authorised publication of the *El País* article, which he had in fact written in 1949. The family had a farm in Santiago de Compostela, where Schmitt would spend his summers with his daughter and grandchildren (Rodríguez Mourullo 2011). On Thursdays, when there was a market in the town, Schmitt could be seen on the corner of the street watching the rustic scene. "With time", recalls sociologist Fermín Bouza, who grew up in the city, "I guessed the meaning of his gaze, which was directed towards nostalgia for rural and medieval Europe, which was already lost" (Bouza 2012).

Long an admirer of the Spanish legal theorist Juan Donoso Cortés, and a devout Catholic, Schmitt's relationship with Spain had been close for decades (Müller 2003, p. 133). Donoso, whose notions of dictatorship and the political decision had influenced Schmitt profoundly, became—thanks to Schmitt's writings—an important source of political thought for intellectuals under Franco's regime, which lasted from 1939 until 1975 (López García 1996, p. 142). During this period Schmitt had come to be seen in Spain as the "last guardian of the 'Great Christian-European Tradition'"

2   *The Schmitt-Podemos connection*

that yoked religion to politics (p. 142); he was enough of an intellectual celebrity that Franco's Information and Tourism minister referred to him as Spain's "buen amigo y maestro" (Müller 2003, p. 134). Soon after a trip to Spain in 1951, Schmitt himself wrote to a friend that he was "still as if numbed by the contrast between the truly wonderful, and also honourable, welcome in Spain and the malicious persecution in my fatherland" (Mehring 2014, p. 450). In the Spain of this era, in turn, Schmitt saw the realisation of a project he had hoped to see come to fruition in Germany but which had been thwarted by the Second World War (Müller 2003, p. 147). "Essentially", writes Schmitt scholar Jan-Werner Müller, "he inverted José Ortega y Gasset's notion that 'Spain is the problem, Europe is the solution'" (Müller 2003, p. 138; cf. Mehring 2014, p. 525).

For some decades after the passage of Spain's Amnesty Law in October 1977 (nine months after the publication of Schmitt's article), it might have seemed as if Schmitt's influence had waned—although, as we will learn in later chapters, the politics of this period remained distinctly Schmittian. Until a few years ago, that is, when various Schmittian concepts began to reappear in Spanish politics: his belief that the will of the people must sometimes override the constitution; his notion that democratic politics must always involve exclusion and the risk of fatal violence; incitements to the release of public passion; and calls for national myths to reinvigorate political practice. The principal agent behind this reappearance was, counterintuitively, the progressive political force known as Podemos ("We Can" in Spanish), which by mid-2016 had become the third largest party in the Spanish parliament after less than three years on the political scene. Podemos' paradoxical revival of Schmittian political thought did not go unnoticed: "until the rise of Podemos", observes professor of constitutional law Javier Tajadura, "no political party has ever assumed—in such a clear and distinct form—Schmitt's doctrine: decisionism" (Tajadura Tejada 2015).

The Schmitt-Podemos paradox

Schmitt's work has been tarnished since the 1930s by his close association with German National Socialism. In the decade after the First World War, the militancy, authoritarianism and anti-pluralism that characterised Nazism rose to the surface of his writing; to any of his readers after this point they would have been unmissable. Yet, soon after the end of the Second World War, the political left began to appropriate his ideas. As early as the late 1960s in Italy, for example, the political philosopher and Communist Party activist Mario Tronti used Carl Schmitt as a corrective to Marxist theory, drawing on his ideas to propose that capitalists be treated as absolute political enemies (cf. Mandarini 2014; Müller 2003, p. 178). But what is

The Schmitt-Podemos connection 3

remarkable about Podemos' more recent appropriation is the consistency with which Schmittian ideas have been integrated into a major political party's programme. Schmitt has not appeared in Podemos' politics merely as a background figure who occasionally contributes to its thinking, as do other political theorists such as Machiavelli. Instead, Schmitt's thought has unmistakably helped to structure Podemos' political performances; it is right there on the surface, brazen and with its edges hardly blunted.

Schmitt is certainly not the only theorist whose ideas have moulded Podemos' political thought. Thinkers on the Left have also exerted a strong influence on the party's intellectual underpinnings. But this fact subtracts nothing from the importance of a Schmittian cosmology to Podemos' politics: Schmitt may not be their most significant intellectual influence, but it is undeniable that—at least during the party's first three years—Schmittian political thought came to play a major role in the way the party's leaders thought about politics. Given the web of memory through which Schmitt's vision of politics is likely to be read in Spain—a web in which Schmitt is tightly entangled with the fascist regime of Francisco Franco and its legacy—this requires further explanation. Our concern is not to present a comprehensive guide to the political theory behind what has become one of the most successful political formations of recent times. Nor is it to assess to what extent Podemos' political behaviour is really Schmittian or not—though the concluding chapter will deal with this question briefly. It is simply to lay out how Schmittian ideas—whether or not they have come directly from Schmitt himself—have shaped the party leaders' political world view, and to ask why they have been able to do so, apparently against significant odds.

As in Tronti's Italy of the 1960s and 1970s, fascism has a recent—and to some extent an ongoing—history in Spain. While few seem aware of the Schmittian juristic justification given to Spain's fascist regime by its intellectuals from the 1930s onwards, or of Schmitt's proximity to the regime after the Second World War, the Schmittian aspects of Francoist politics continue to be discussed and condemned by those on the political Left even when they are not labelled as such. Yet the young Podemos' patriotism verging on nationalism, its bellicose metaphors, and its veneration of strong leadership all bear traces of the same kind of politics, which Spain has apparently worked so hard to eradicate. If these ideas do not recall the dictatorship itself, then they certainly revive many of the themes of the Civil War that preceded it, which after the 1977 amnesty Spain's political class made such a performance of forgetting.

Part of the story here, no doubt, is about "self-positioning" and "branding" (Baert, 2015, pp. 158–189) in that the Podemos intellectuals have drawn in part on a Schmittian perspective to locate themselves (some

4 *The Schmitt-Podemos connection*

would say, rather skilfully) within the Spanish political context, presenting a radical agenda that ostensibly moves beyond the traditional left-right divide. In what follows, we shall uncover how their self-positioning has taken place very much through the "positioning" of others, relying on sharp juxtapositions: the intellectuals involved have portrayed the group they call "*la casta*" (the so-called political elite) as the enemy, the transition from Franco's dictatorship to democracy as a charade, liberal democracy as a smokescreen, and so on. We shall also learn, however, that the political context in which Podemos' leaders currently operate is not simply "given": it is also one that they have helped to create and maintain. Indeed, the very same writings and speeches in which they elaborate on their political stances also depict their political context as one that is politically depleted—one that calls for the resurrection of the kind of heroism associated with an earlier period in Spanish history. Podemos has been particularly persuasive in providing a new depiction of contemporary Spanish politics and of its recent history. In this book, we will explore this unique political imaginary which allowed for the reconciliation of *prima facie* conflicting political positions. What we will not do, however, is evaluate how far this imaginary and its positioning effects have contributed to Podemos' success. Our intention is not to explain Podemos' impressive trajectory through the political sphere, analysing its reconfiguration of Spain's political party structure; others have taken up this task (see Ramiro and Gómez 2017; Ferrada Stoehrel 2017). It is to account for an intriguing segment of its leaders' trajectory through the realm of ideas.

To use the term "positioning", as we just did, is not to suggest that Podemos' leaders are always craftily and cynically manipulating their audiences or that privately they hold very different (and possibly opposing) views to the ones they publicly profess. Of course, given the nature of their activities, there *has* been an element of political manoeuvring, with the occasional discrepancy between private convictions and public utterances. Especially their positioning beyond the traditional left-right divide—or, to put it differently, their avoidance of a leftist label—is at least partly strategic. As our story unfolds, however, it will quickly become apparent that the main protagonists seem remarkably committed to and emotionally entangled with the stances they take and that their trajectories indicate a continuity (and, to some extent, authenticity) of their political views that cannot simply be ignored. Therefore, an exclusively instrumental-rational reading of their writings and speeches would be thoroughly misguided.

This, then, poses the question how and why Podemos took up this Schmittian tradition of political thought during the party's infancy, given that it is redolent of a bellicose far-right politics and that its principal exponent was so closely associated with Nazism. To answer this question

The Schmitt-Podemos connection 5

we will focus on the period between the party's inception in 2014 and its second Citizen Assembly in February 2017, when the influence of Schmittian thought on Podemos' rhetoric was at its clearest. Our investigation will take us into both Spanish and German history, and into the intellectual hinterland of Podemos' leaders. It will take us into the theory and strategy behind a populist political party built for the twenty-first century and its institutions—an agent capable, if its leaders are to be believed, of reversing the bleak prognosis commentators have been handing down to the European left for years. It will also, briefly, bring us to the question of what it is to be a young European today, and specifically to the question of what it is to be a young academic in today's European universities. Beyond these narrative landmarks, which make for an interesting story in their own right, investigating the apparent paradox of Schmitt's reincarnation in contemporary Spain brings us to four further questions, the first pair more general—from the sociology of ideas and political theory—and the second pair quite specific.

The sociology of ideas poses the question of how readers who would have vehemently rejected the politics implied by a theory in its original context come to adopt the theory none the less. Just as it is fascinating how exponents of the French Nouvelle Droite such as Alain de Benoist have been adopting Gramscian theory (whilst unmistakably rejecting Gramsci's political agenda), it is intriguing how key figures in Podemos came to flirt with Schmittian political theory. This poses a question about resonance: how has Schmittian political theory been able to resonate so strongly with these readers that its original implications have not hindered its appropriation? The answer is that the filter through which Podemos' leaders view Spanish politics makes contemporary reality appear much more like Weimar Germany, the original context in which Schmitt was writing, than it may seem to us. This filter takes the form of a narrative in which personal and political stories are woven together—a narrative that extends into both Spain's past and its future. It is a narrative that draws on cultural structures at play in Spanish politics for over a century, resulting in a patterning homologous to that which runs through Schmitt's political theory. Homology of narrative structures is the key to understanding how Schmittian ideas have managed to resonate with leaders of a progressive political party a century later (see Alexander and Smith 2005). While the polarity of the narrative elements within these structures may be different, similarities between the structures themselves have in this case been sufficient for resonance to occur.

Because the Podemos leaders' narrative connects the personal and the political, and because it extends into the future as well as the past, it tells a story not just about a prospective political transformation but about a prospective personal transformation as well. It is partly because Schmittian

6 *The Schmitt-Podemos connection*

theory echoes the part of the Podemos leaders' narrative that deals with personal transformation that it has successfully resonated with them—not just because it echoes the part that deals with Spain's political transformation (though as we will see, to distinguish two different "parts" in this way, while analytically useful here, is probably misleading). Theories should be understood to attract readers not just because of their perceived accuracy, but because they appear to promise a desired personal transformation (cf. Isaac 2009, pp. 406–408). By thinking and acting in accordance with a new theory, by beginning to perform their life according to its script, readers can, or so it may seem, change their form of life. Quite significant inaccuracies and even damning associations may be passed over if a theory offers sufficient performative pull. For the Podemos intellectuals, living through Schmittian political theory promises to end the boredom and frustration produced both by the immediate milieu of academia and by liberal politics. The script of Schmitt's theory suggests a dramatic life that takes up where their ancestors, who fought against Franco, left off, and continues the epic in which they were protagonists. When combined with its structural fit with Podemos' narrative about Spanish politics, the performative pull of Schmitt's decisionism has been too strong to resist.

One of the central claims in what follows is that intellectual currents or ideas in general are more likely to resonate with people if they can be incorporated into compelling individual narratives. In two other sociohistorical studies of public intellectuals, we have come across a similar phenomenon. Firstly, *The Existentialist Moment* showed how in the 1940s Jean-Paul Sartre's writings—his philosophy, novels, plays, journalistic pieces and public lectures—managed to resonate with sections of the French public because they spoke directly to their recent experiences. Sartre's writings and speeches provided a vocabulary to make sense of the trauma of the war, helping to draw a line underneath it and move forward (Baert 2015). Secondly, a recent socio-historical study on the Black Consciousness Movement revealed how in the 1970s Steve Biko's interventions were remarkably compelling and struck a chord with Black South Africans partly because he was particularly skilful in linking his political agenda to their everyday lives. His political views were not simply abstract formulations— they were intimately connected to his own biography and that of millions of others (Morgan and Baert, 2017). In both cases—the study of Sartre and Biko—new theoretical articulations were linked to the notion of rebirth, with a *tabula rasa* enabling the conception of new societal and political projects as well as new biographies. We shall find that Podemos and Schmittian thought follow similar patterns.

Political theory, meanwhile, poses the question of the nature of populism. Much has been written claiming that populism is inevitably a sinister

The Schmitt-Podemos connection 7

mode of doing politics: that a return to populism is a return to the horrors of the 1930s. By peering directly into the darkest part of Podemos' politics, the part influenced by Schmitt, we can test what some have claimed is an innocuous, even positive, incarnation of populism. Does this focus on Podemos' Schmittian seam reveal something sinister within the poster party of the European populist left? Or does it instead show that in the right hands even the worst aspects of populism can be transformed into something to be embraced, rather than feared?

In his book on populism, Schmitt scholar Jan-Werner Müller argues that the phenomenon should be understood in Schmittian terms. Müller defines populism as "a particular moralistic imagination of politics, a way of perceiving the political world that sets a morally pure and fully unified ... people against elites who are deemed corrupt or in some other way morally inferior" (Müller 2016, p. 20). Podemos' imagination of politics certainly corresponds to this definition. Yet Müller goes on to characterise populists as anti-pluralist (p. 20), as hostile towards real participation by citizens (p. 29), and as prone to internal authoritarianism (p. 36). Schmitt would have approved of this kind of populism, and it is because of this that, as Müller writes, Schmitt's work "served as a conceptual bridge from democracy to nondemocracy" (p. 28). But has Podemos taken up these Schmittian elements of populism, in which case might it too be the bridge from democracy to nondemocracy in Spain?

The answer is not straightforward. Though he mentions that Podemos has been labelled "populist" Müller does not have much beyond that to say about the party. He does, however, suggest that despite their anti-elitism the precursor movement to Podemos, the *indignados*, were not "actual populists" because they were not a part of the population claiming to represent the whole—and that distinguishing non-populist anti-elitist political actors from populist ones "is a prime task for a theory of populism in Europe today" (Müller 2016, p. 98). The fact that Podemos has drawn directly on Schmitt provides an unparalleled opportunity to see precisely how far this self-described "populist" phenomenon does correspond to the pessimistic definition espoused by political theorists such as Müller, for whom real populism is "a constant peril" (p. 11).

Aside from having a bearing on these general questions from intellectual history and political theory, studying Schmitt's reincarnation in twenty-first century Spain is an effective way of answering two more specific questions about the nature of present political reality. First, because it allows us to get at what kind of political formation Podemos really is. Looking at an extreme and unexpected part of a phenomenon helps us to understand its essence, because it pushes us to investigate its deepest roots. If we are initially surprised to find Schmitt among Podemos' intellectual influences, then it is because what we already know about Podemos jars with what we

8 *The Schmitt-Podemos connection*

know about Schmitt. Unpicking the puzzle will lead us far beyond the surface Podemos presents externally to its intellectual and emotional core.

Assessing how well Schmitt's ideas have travelled in contemporary Spain also provides an opportunity to compare a twenty-first-century liberal-democratic society against the Weimar Republic in some detail. Just as Schmitt's political theory was a response to the deficiencies he detected in the German politics of the time, Podemos' integration of his ideas into its own political strategy is a response to its diagnosis of contemporary European liberal democracy. Schmitt scholars such as Ellen Kennedy have suggested that if we have something to learn from Schmitt then this is partly because Weimar Germany is not so different from our own societies (Kennedy, 2004, p. 7). Schmitt's analysis of the Weimar Republic was acute; he anticipated problems that his contemporaries missed. Perhaps his theory can similarly reveal things about our societies today that are all too easy to pass over. In the thought of Podemos' intellectuals we find a sophisticated application of Schmitt's ideas to our political institutions. Even if this application is excessively bleak, it is likely to be instructive.

Introducing Podemos

On 15 May 2011 the public square at Spain's symbolic centre, the Puerta del Sol in Madrid, filled with people protesting against the Government's programme of economic austerity. The policies of the governing Partido Socialista Obrero Español (PSOE—Spanish Socialist Workers' Party) had left large swathes of the population unemployed, and protests against the eviction of homeowners unable to keep up their mortgage repayments had been gaining momentum for months. The events of "15-M", as these protests came to be known, were the trigger for Podemos' formation. On that day Íñigo Errejón, who would later become Podemos' chief political strategist, arrived back in Madrid from a year of fieldwork in Bolivia (Tremlett 2015). Errejón was in the final stages of his doctoral study in the Department of Sociology and Political Science at the Complutense University of Madrid. While at the Complutense he had become friends with a young professor, Pablo Iglesias, known for his success in popularizing political theory. Iglesias would later become Podemos' leader.

Though Iglesias and Errejón were academics, they had been political activists before becoming political scientists (Iglesias 2015a, p. 152). All their political experience was on the left. Both had spent time as advisors to the left-wing party Izquierda Unida (United Left) (p. 165) and were also part of a left-wing think tank, the Fundación Centro de Estudios Políticos y Sociales, which had advised Latin American administrations. Both had experienced leftist activism abroad—Errejón in Bolivia and Iglesias in Italy

(p. 164). Iglesias was even named after the first leader of the Socialist Workers' Party, the PSOE. What Iglesias, Errejón and their closest colleagues at the Complutense shared was both a belief in left-wing politics and a belief that its twentieth-century European incarnation had failed. What was needed was, as Perry Anderson had argued, "a stance of uncompromising realism" (Iglesias 2015b, p. 8n). Left-wing politics had for too long been driven—and, more importantly, held back—by unsubstantiated Marxian assumptions about both the course that history would take and the causal mechanisms behind history's making.

For a group of political scientists frustrated with the detachment of academic work from real political activity, 15-M presented itself as an opportunity. Influenced by the work of Argentinian political theorist Ernesto Laclau, Errejón and Iglesias saw in 15-M what they call, in Gramscian terms, a "situation of organic crisis" of the Spanish political regime (Iglesias 2015a, p. 165). The political status quo that their youthful political experience had taught them to be inadequate was finally showing not just signs of weakness, but signs of weakness that they themselves could exploit. What followed was a campaign to change the terms of debate in Spanish politics. At first the vehicle for this campaign was a television talk show presented by Iglesias, which the Complutense academics used as a springboard from which to "cross enemy lines" onto right-wing debate programmes (Iglesias quoted in Tremlett 2015). As their reach expanded and their faces became known to more of the TV-viewing Spanish population, the prospect of their leading a mainstream political party became more realistic. Almost three years after the 15-M protests, on the 17th of January 2014, Podemos was founded.

Podemos was established with the belief that democracy as it currently exists in Spain is of an impoverished sort; the party's strongest message is that democracy must be deepened. For Podemos this meant achieving genuine "popular sovereignty" (Errejón and Mouffe 2016, p. 115) of the kind that would see significant redistribution of wealth from those who had "ignored the social contract, put themselves above the law" to ordinary people (pp. 107–108). One of Podemos' headline proposals was the proper application of article 128 of the Constitution, which states that all the country's wealth should be subordinated to the general interest (Iglesias 2014b).

In Podemos' analysis, Spanish democracy had been fundamentally undermined from both inside and outside the country. Beyond Spain's borders, Germany exercised a form of "financial totalitarianism" over the rest of the EU member states (Iglesias 2015c, 14:08). It was able to do this because of the EU's institutional make-up, which requires "European populations to submit themselves to institutions that they have not elected" (Iglesias 2015a, p. 170). By going along with the EU's diktats, which when stripped of their thin Euro-varnish were exposed as those of the

10 *The Schmitt-Podemos connection*

German chancellery, elites within other countries—and particularly those of the European periphery such as Spain—gave their "collaborationist support" (p. 170) to a new project of German hegemony (p. 102); they renounced the sovereignty of their people without their consent (p. 170). The result was a division of labour that favoured German financial interests and condemned the countries of the Southern European periphery to poverty and shame.

While Germany lay at one end of Podemos' axis of enmity, at the other end was the Spanish political elite. This was an elite that in Podemos' view had consistently governed in favour of the wealthiest in society and at the expense of everyone else. It did so because it was "substantively corrupt" (Iglesias 2014a, p. 155); thanks to "revolving doors" between politics and big business, politicians have an incentive to favour companies that might employ them as directors after they leave office (Iglesias 2015a, p. 127). This system effectively "allows those who have not presented themselves at elections to govern" (Iglesias 2014a, p. 156). But it was not just the financial elites who were privileged by corruption; there was something deeper and more peculiarly Spanish going on here. One of the most salient examples of corruption that Iglesias cited was that of a judicial system that refused to investigate the crimes of the Franco dictatorship. The one judge who had tried to do this, Baltasar Garzón, was himself put on trial (Iglesias 2015a, p. 157; Graham 2012, p. 148).

Podemos referred to the elites in charge of Spanish politics—both those who are formally speaking politicians and those who are not, but who wield political power—as "*la casta*". The term was taken from a 2007 book by journalists Sergio Rizzo and Gian Antonio Stella about the Italian political elites and their greed (Rizzo and Stella 2007); though Berlusconi wore his corruption much more visibly on his sleeve, Podemos wished to signal that the Spanish elites, with current President and leader of the Partido Popular (PP—People's Party) Mariano Rajoy at their head, were not much better. Complicit in the success of the *casta* were not just the politicians of the conservative PP—the main party of the elites and of corruption—but also those of the socialist PSOE and the centrist liberal Ciudadanos (Citizens) party. It was the PSOE that, in Podemos' view, had given up on social democracy towards the end of Zapatero's administration, "delivering itself to the suicide of the Third Way". Meanwhile Ciudadanos represented nothing other than a scheme to renew the current elites (Iglesias 2015a, p. 69). Whether they were members of the *casta* or not (the Podemos intellectuals deliberately avoided defining precisely who was part of this disgraced company (Errejón and Mouffe 2016, p. 133)), the alternatives at the ballot box were merely accessories to the *casta*'s rule.

Though these were Podemos' immediate political adversaries, Iglesias and Errejón told a longer history that set the party at odds not just with current elites but with the Spanish political establishment more broadly understood. The transition to democracy that followed Franco's death in 1975 was, in Podemos' view, deeply inadequate. Errejón refers to it as a form of "passive revolution" in which ordinary people were included, but in a subordinate role. What happened after 1975 was not a process led by "the people", but rather one orchestrated by the very same elites—the "oligarchies"—that had flourished under *el franquismo*" (Francoism). Unsurprisingly the oligarchies steered the Transition in a direction that was to their own benefit, introducing a regime that allowed them to remain "practically intact" to this day. Though they had left the Constitution of 1978 almost untouched, the Spanish oligarchies had "emptied the social accord of 78 of its democratic controls and guarantees", ensuring that those "in the apex of the pyramid" could accumulate wealth and power undisturbed (Errejón and Mouffe 2015). After 30 years, the arrangement orchestrated by the oligarchies had come "to appear as a natural political order, harmonious, the only one possible". Podemos wished to disrupt this appearance. Only by doing so would it achieve a new transition, a new pact, in which the fundamental protagonists were not the political or economic elites but the people (Iglesias 2015a, p. 82).

On the basis of this analysis of Spanish politics Podemos, as Iglesias wrote for an English-speaking audience, advocated "sovereign processes that would limit the power of finance, spur the transformation of production, ensure a wider redistribution of wealth and push for a more democratic configuration of European institutions" (Iglesias 2015b, p. 10). It sought to reverse the modus operandi whereby the country was governed in favour of the financial elites; in Iglesias' words, "You cannot govern for both millionaires at the top of society and for the majority of ordinary people; it's simply not possible" (Iglesias, 2015d, 10:00). "[T]he democratisation of the economy" was, according to Iglesias, Podemos' principal objective (Iglesias, 2015a, p. 57). Labour legislation must be changed, since it currently "encourages temporariness, precariousness and the destruction of jobs" (p. 60). Small and medium enterprises, rather than huge corporations, should have greater support from the state (p. 61). Corruption must be halted, since citizens suffered as a result of "daily fraud" (Iglesias, 2015a, p. 59; Iglesias, 2014d, 17:22). And against the German project Podemos wished to catalyse "a European civil society that demands the social and democratic foundations of the European dream left to us by antifascism" (Iglesias, 2015a, p. 50).

Podemos' approach to politics

As the Podemos intellectuals saw it, 15-M signalled not a crisis of the state, because state institutions remained able to fulfil their functions, but a crisis

12 *The Schmitt-Podemos connection*

of the regime (Errejón 2015a; Errejón and Mouffe 2016, p. 48). They began to recognise in 15-M what Gramsci called an "organic crisis", explained by political theorists Ernesto Laclau and Chantal Mouffe—through whose theoretical lens Errejón at least viewed events—as "[a] conjuncture where there is a generalised weakening of the relational system defining the identities of a given social or political space, and where, as a result there is a proliferation of floating elements" (Laclau and Mouffe 2014, p. 122).

To understand why the crisis signalled by 15-M was so significant for Errejón and Iglesias, we must understand their constructivist perspective on politics. Heavily influenced by Laclau and Mouffe, this view of politics goes one step further than Gramsci in its revision of Marxist thinking. Gramsci emphasised that the dominance of any given political regime depended on a shared set of ideas and values being able to construct a "collective will" that could glue the regime together (Laclau and Mouffe 2014, pp. 57–63). It was not enough for a class such as the proletariat to take state power in its neat form, as it was for Marx, simply by virtue of its economic position; moral and intellectual leadership was needed on top of this to produce a set of ideas and values—of *meanings*—that would bind a number of different sectors together in a collaboration capable of sustaining the regime. If this was done, a class could become a "hegemonic subject" and govern in its own interest.

But whereas Gramsci believed that any collective will needed to be constructed around an existing, economically-defined class, Laclau and Mouffe dispense with this vestige of "essentialism" (Laclau and Mouffe 2014, p. 124). They propose the thoroughly constructivist view that there is no foundation that the collective will need necessarily be constructed upon; the ideas and values around which such a will might be constructed are consequently not limited to those that have a special relationship to pre-existing classes. The "articulatory practices" of moral and intellectual leadership have free rein when it comes to gluing together a political regime. By infusing the world with meanings, they may be able to turn any combination of people—not necessarily with a particular "class" at their centre—into a "hegemonic subject" able to dominate politics.

In political systems such as Spain's, "an actor is hegemonic", as Errejón notes, "when it has constructed a 'national-popular collective will' (Gramsci) or a general interest that allows it to present its demands and political project as to the benefit of the whole political community or its large majority" (Errejón 2011a, p. 9; Iglesias 2015a, p. 63). In Spain it was not, in Podemos' view, a particular class that exercised hegemony, but rather *la casta*. What 15-M demonstrated was that the set of meanings (the ideas and values) that glued together the *casta*'s regime was beginning to lose its hold. Some of the key terms employed by this story had been emptied of their meaning—they were thus "floating elements", signifiers

The Schmitt-Podemos connection 13

that could be re-filled with meaning conducive to Podemos' aims. No longer was the current order able to "naturalise itself", to "appear as the only possibility" (Errejón and Mouffe 2016, p. 46). From the perspective of those who assume "the autonomy of the political" (Errejón 2015a, p. 23), like Laclau and Mouffe and, following them, the Podemos leaders, 15-M was an indication that strategic cultural intervention could help bring about regime change. Although the majority of those camping out in the Puerta del Sol protests were part of the so-called Facebook generation, the Podemos leaders recognised that behind the protesters was a much larger audience of sympathisers who were following events at home on television (Iglesias 2015a, p. 105). Many of these people were frustrated because austerity policies had denied them the standard of living they had come to expect (p. 141); what resonated with them was "the main component of a new common sense" that the 15-M protests "put on the table", a "rejection of the dominant political and economic elites, systematically signalled as corrupt" (Iglesias 2015b, p. 12). These were not people who had been members of political parties or political activists in the past; they had been "politically socialized through television", and as such were not "'representable' within the traditional left-right categories of the political space" (p. 17). The new story that Podemos needed to tell was one in which the elites were the adversary of the people united as a whole, undivided by left-right divisions. *La gente* (the people) was the audience on the other side of the television screen, against whom the state had been set to work by the governing *casta* (Iglesias 2015c, 7:00).

This opposition between the people and the governing *casta* had immediate resonance for the Podemos intellectuals, for whom Latin America's "gained decade" was an important reference point. In countries such as Venezuela and Bolivia, populist movements had overthrown entrenched elites, bringing economic prosperity to a large part of the population who had gained nothing from years of obedience to neoclassical economic doctrine. At this point the Podemos intellectuals began to talk about the prospect of Southern Europe's "latinamericanization"—the possibility that populism of the kind that had swept Venezuela and Bolivia might be cultivated in countries such as Spain (Iglesias 2015b, p. 14). The Argentinian Ernesto Laclau, a major influence on Íñigo Errejón, had used the Latin American experience to imagine possible populist futures for the European left; now Errejón did the same (Errejón and Mouffe 2016, p. 131).

Although both their political experience and their intellectual influences were predominantly on the left, Iglesias and Errejón believed that if they were to construct a "new common sense" it would have to locate itself beyond the left-right axis. It was not just that the majority of the audience they wished to reach was neither decidedly on the left nor decidedly on the

14 *The Schmitt-Podemos connection*

right; it was also that a bipolar party system was one of the emblems of the 1975–78 period of transition that had allowed the pre-Transition elites to remain in place. It had done so by dividing the people into two, setting them against each other rather than against those who had been at the apex of the pyramid under Franco's autocracy and continued undisturbed by democracy. By defining itself along the left-right continuum, any political movement would place itself within the set of ideas and values that had kept the current regime in place (Iglesias 2014c, 8:00). It would be construed as just another political formation operating within the system in opposition to half of the population (the "right"), one whose motivations could therefore be understood *a priori* (Iglesias 2015a, p. 77). The Podemos intellectuals needed to resist this.

What any successful political force needed to do was to "fight for the 'terms of the conversation'" (Iglesias 2015b, p. 16), to "reorder and redraw" the discursive terrain on which politics is conducted (Errejón and Mouffe 2016, p. 57). By doing so—by rejecting the terms "left/right", for instance—it would be possible to take up a position at "the centre of the board" (p. 57), resisting the immediately alienating effect of being positioned at one end or the other of an existing horizontal axis split evenly in two. The terms "left/right" would be replaced by the terms "above/below", with "above" signifying not half of a vertical axis, but that minute portion at the very top occupied by the elites. "Below" referred to by far the largest portion of the vertical axis, the part occupied by "the people".

Fighting for "the terms of the conversation" was something at which the Podemos leaders, after years marinating in elite universities, excelled. "Fundamentally", as Errejón concedes, "we are artisans who work with words" (Errejón 2015b, 28:45) Following the 15-M protests, they began to establish new channels through which to conduct this fight. But at this stage a political party in the traditional sense was not the leaders' priority. In their view it was not primarily through political parties that people engaged in politics, but rather through the media. If the Podemos leaders' priority had been to court the Facebook generation who had pitched up in their thousands to protest in the Puerta del Sol, they might have turned to social media, but their ambitions were greater than this (cf. Iglesias 2015a, p. 165). And so Iglesias began to present *La Tuerka* (The Screw), a political talk show on "the most fundamental terrain of ideological production: television" (Iglesias 2015b, p. 14). "Television", Iglesias would later write,

> conditions and even helps to manufacture the frameworks through which people think—the mental structures and their associated values—at a much higher level of intensity than the traditional sites of ideological production: family, school, religion. As far as political

attitudes and opinions are concerned, in Spain TV talk shows are probably the major producers of arguments explicitly for popular use ... In the context of the crisis ... as far as specifically political debates are concerned, TV studios have become the real parliaments.

(Iglesias 2015b, p. 16)

Although it was not fighting directly for seats in parliament, Iglesias and his colleagues saw *La Tuerka* as a political party nonetheless (Iglesias 2015b, p. 14). Political parties are communications media, they reasoned; rather than being a member of the PP or the PSOE, most people are a member "of *El País*, of *La Razón*, of *El Mundo*" (all Spanish newspapers) (Iglesias 2015a, p. 95). These media were the contemporary version of Gramsci's "organic intellectuals", responsible for presenting the bundle of ideas and values that would form the cement of political regimes. It was therefore no exaggeration to say that "reality is created" through these media (p. 164). Lacking their own discrete channel—their own television station or newspaper that would launch them immediately into the role of organic intellectual—the Podemos leaders approached *La Tuerka* as a "training camp". By practising on the platform provided by *La Tuerka* they could develop a distinctive "style" which would later enable them to hijack slots on other media channels, using them to constitute themselves as a collective organic intellectual (p. 95).

A thoroughgoing constructivism, reminiscent of that proposed by Laclau and Mouffe, is evident in this strategy. In contrast with the "essentialism" of the left—and even of Gramsci—the Podemos leaders thought it "idiotic" to assume that a political movement needed to be constructed from below. "[P]recisely because we come from where we come from", Iglesias wrote—perhaps in reference to academia, perhaps to Spain itself—"we are clear that institutions transform society. This is something that the right has taught us" (Iglesias 2015a, p. 106). Indeed, in Iglesias' view, Podemos' political style could be encapsulated in the lemma: "If you want to get it right, don't do what the left would do" (Iglesias 2014a, p. 10). It is not, then, just that characterising themselves as "left" would do discursive damage to their attempt to position themselves at the centre of the political board; it is also that their approach to politics itself is not wholly of the left—it has something of the right about it. A political movement does not need to be fomented gradually from the bottom up; "[i]t can be constructed in a *Blitz*" from above (Iglesias 2015a, p. 106).

The rise of Podemos

At its base, Podemos' party structure echoes that of the 15-M movement; it has been designed to allow the greatest possible number of people to

16 *The Schmitt-Podemos connection*

participate in making decisions about policy. Two horizontal branches of the organisation, Circles and the Citizen Assembly, exist alongside each other. They are capped by an 81-member Citizen Council, co-ordinated by a single secretary-general.

Equivalent to 15-M's neighbourhood associations, Circles are clusters of politically like-minded people affiliated to Podemos who share a territorial region, profession or an interest in a particular issue addressed by the party's manifesto. They are the basic unit of the Podemos machine, designed to produce political nourishment for the party by proposing initiatives and topics for debate. The Circles—which have been set up around Spain, but also in countries as distant as Norway and Paraguay—are connected by Podemos' multiple online discussion and decision-making platforms in a digital-analogue hybrid web (Podemos 2016, pp. 7–11).

The Citizen Assembly, which meets at least once every three years, is made up of all Podemos' members. All major decisions are made by the Assembly, in which every member's voice and vote is equal. It falls to the Assembly to make the final decision about Podemos' general political direction; to draw up electoral lists through primaries; to approve or reject any pact or alliance with other national parties; to elect or dismiss the secretary-general and the Citizen Council—the executive body responsible for the party's political management (pp. 13–16). Podemos' secretary-general presides over the council, assuming responsibility for the co-ordination of its various executive functions (p. 17).

Twenty-four hours after Podemos' official launch on 17 January 2014, the fledgling party had secured the 50,000 supporting signatories Iglesias had declared necessary to contest the forthcoming European Parliament election (El Periódico 2014). In the May 2014 EU elections, just four months after Podemos was founded, the party won 7.97% of the vote, gaining five seats. Regional elections in Andalucía the following year were even more successful. Two months later, in May 2015, Podemos-backed alliances swept to power in Madrid and Barcelona, installing candidates linked (though not actually belonging) to the party in the two most significant mayoralties in Spain. In the general elections of December 2015 Podemos, now in alliance with regional parties with similar political platforms, won 20.66% of the vote, only one percentage point less than the PSOE.

Less than two years after its birth, Podemos had succeeded in breaking open the two-party system that had settled into its stride not long after Franco's death and had lasted more than thirty years. Spain now faced a political impasse: the PP had suffered heavily in the election, losing its majority in parliament, but remained the largest party with 28.7% of the vote. The PSOE had also lost ground, but as the largest party on the left it remained the party with the best prospects for forming a governing

The Schmitt-Podemos connection 17

coalition. At one point Podemos agreed in principle to govern alongside the PSOE, but talks soon became acrimonious and any hope of a left-wing government evaporated. New general elections were called for June 2016. This time Podemos decided to join forces with other minor national parties such as Izquierda Unida, as well as smaller regional parties, in the hope of achieving a *sorpasso* (overtaking) of the PSOE. The electoral coalition Unidos Podemos (United We Can) was announced in May 2016. Though the attempted *sorpasso* failed—and in fact the coalition gained over a million votes fewer than Podemos had won in 2015—Unidos Podemos held on to its title as Spain's third party and retained its seats in parliament. Meanwhile the PP walked away from the June 2016 elections significantly strengthened, enabling its leader Rajoy to form another PP government at the end of October 2016.

References

Alexander, Jeffrey and Philip Smith. 2005. "The Strong Program in Cultural Sociology: Elements of a Structural Hermeneutics". In *The Meanings of Social Life: A Cultural Sociology* Edited by Jeffrey Alexander. New York: Oxford University Press.

Baert, Patrick. 2015. *The Existentialist Moment: The Rise of Sartre as a Public Intellectual*. Cambridge: Polity.

Bouza, Fermín. 2012. "Galicia y la mirada de Carl". *El País*, 13 September.

El Periódico. 2014. "Pablo Iglesias consigue en un día los 50.000 apoyos que pedía para seguir adelante con Podemos". www.elperiodico.com, 19 January. Last accessed 27 February 2018.

Errejón, Íñigo. 2011a. "¿Qué es el análisis político? Una propuesta desde la teoría del discurso y la hegemonía". *Revista Estudiantil Latinoamericana de Ciencias Sociales.*

Errejón, Íñigo. 2015a. "Pateando el tablero: 'El 15M como discurso contra-hegemónico' cuatro años después: Entrevista con Íñigo Errejón". *Encrucijadas. Revista Crítica de Ciencias Sociales*, 9. pp. 1–35.

Errejón, Íñigo. 2015b. "Podemos ya ha ganado las próximas elecciones generales en España". Video available at www.youtube.com/watch?v=aGnbl0sRl-E. Last accessed 16 February 2017.

Errejón, Íñigo and Chantal Mouffe. 2015. "Diálogo entre Íñigo Errejón y Chantal Mouffe". *La Circular*, 3 August. Available at http://lacircular.info/dialogo-en tre-inigo-errejon-y-chantal-mouffe/. Last accessed 27 February 2018.

Errejón, Íñigo and Chantal Mouffe. 2016. *Podemos: In the Name of the People.* London: Lawrence & Wishart.

Ferrada Stoehrel, Rodrigo. 2017. "The regime's worst nightmare: the mobilization of citizen democracy. A study of Podemos' (aesthetic) populism and the production of affect in political discourse". *Cultural Studies* 31:4. pp. 543–579.

18 *The Schmitt-Podemos connection*

Graham, Helen. 2012. *The War and its Shadow: Spain's Civil War in Europe's Long Twentieth Century*. Brighton: Sussex Academic Press.

Iglesias, Pablo. 2014a. *Disputar la democracia: política para tiempos de crisis*. Madrid: Ediciones Akal.

Iglesias, Pablo. 2014b. "Pablo Iglesias anuncia su intención de presentarse a la elecciones europeas". *Las Mañanas de Cuatro*, 14 January. Available at www.cuatro.com/las-mananas-de-cuatro/Pablo-Iglesias-intencion-presentarse-e lecciones_2_1732530095.html. Last accessed 27 February 2018.

Iglesias, Pablo. 2014c. "Discurso de Pablo Iglesias en Barcelona". Video available at www.youtube.com/watch?v=lvd28BuFAJY. Last accessed 16 February 2017.

Iglesias, Pablo. 2014d. "Discurso de Pablo Iglesias en Vista Alegre". Video available at www.youtube.com/watch?v=aRUp42NjghE. Last accessed 16 February 2017.

Iglesias, Pablo. 2015a. *Una nueva Transición: materiales del año del cambio*. Second Edition. Madrid: Ediciones Akal.

Iglesias, Pablo. 2015b. "Understanding Podemos". *New Left Review* 93 (May-June). pp. 7–22.

Iglesias, Pablo. 2015c. "Discurso de Pablo Iglesias en la Puerta del Sol". Video available at www.youtube.com/watch?v=oe-bJXZ_KGk. Last accessed 16 February 2017.

Iglesias, Pablo. 2015d. "Discurso de Pablo Iglesias en Zaragoza". Video available at www.youtube.com/watch?v=lvd28BuFAJY. Last accessed 16 February 2017.

Isaac, Joel. 2009. "Tangled Loops: Theory, History and the Human Sciences in Modern America". *Modern Intellectual History* 6. pp. 397–424.

Kennedy, Ellen. 2004. *Constitutional Failure: Carl Schmitt in Weimar*. Durham, NC and London: Duke University Press.

Laclau, Ernesto and Chantal Mouffe. 2014. *Hegemony and Socialist Strategy: Towards a Radical Democratic Politics*. London: Verso.

López García, José Antonio. 1996. "La presencia de Carl Schmitt en España". *Revista de Estudios Políticos*, 91. pp. 139–168.

Mandarini, Matteo. 2014. "Notes on the Political Over the Longue Durée". *Viewpoint Magazine*, 2 September.

Mehring, Reinhard. 2014. *Carl Schmitt: A Biography*. Translated by Daniel Steuer. Cambridge: Polity Press.

Morgan, Marcus and Patrick Baert. 2017. "Acting out ideas: performative citizenship in the Black Consciousness Movement". *American Journal of Cultural Sociology*. OnlineFirst, doi:10.1057/s41290–41017–0030–0031.

Müller, Jan-Werner. 2003. *A Dangerous Mind: Carl Schmitt in Post-War European Thought*. New Haven, CT: Yale University Press.

Podemos. 2016. Principios Organizativos. Available at https://podemos.info/wp-content/uploads/2016/11/Principios_organizativos_castellano.pdf. Last accessed 27 February 2018.

Ramiro, Luis and Raúl Gómez. 2017. "Radical-Left Populism during the Great Recession: Podemos and Its Competition with the Established Radical Left". *Political Studies* 65:1S. pp. 108–126.

The Schmitt-Podemos connection 19

Rizzo, Sergio and Gian Antonio Stella. 2007. *La Casta: Cosí i politici italiani sono diventati intoccabili*. Milan: Rizzoli.

Rodríguez Mourullo, Gonzalo. 2011. "Recuerdos de ayer, preocupaciones de hoy". *Revista jurídica de la Universidad Autónoma de Madrid*, 22. pp. 223–246.

Schmitt, Carl. 1977. "Amnistía es la fuerza de olvidar". *El País*, 21 January.

Tajadura Tejada, Javier. 2015. "Peligro de regresión democrática". *El Correo*, 31 January.

Tremlett, Giles. 2015. "The Podemos revolution: how a small group of radical academics changed European politics". *The Guardian*, 31 March.

2 Podemos' encounter with Schmitt

In the months following Germany's defeat at the end of the Second World War, Carl Schmitt remained in Berlin as the city fell into disorder. In August 1945, he wrote a legal opinion on "The International Crime of the War of Aggression". "The atrocities in the special sense that were committed before the last world war and during this war", Schmitt wrote, "must indeed be regarded as '*mala in se*'. Their inhumanity is so great and so evident that it suffices to establish the facts and their perpetrators in order to ground criminal liability without any regard for hitherto existing positive laws" (Mehring 2014, p. 409). According to Schmitt's definition, the perpetrators were those with "access to the political leadership". As the advisor of an advisor to Hitler's inner circle, with no direct access to the Nazi regime's core, Schmitt considered himself excluded from this ignominious band (pp. 410–411).

On 26 September Schmitt was arrested by the Americans, interrogated, and taken to a series of detention camps. He would not be released for more than a year. Because he had been a member of the National Socialist party, he was told at the end of 1945 that he could no longer work in German universities (Mehring 2014, p. 409). In March 1947 he was taken to Nuremberg, where he was interned for five weeks and interrogated four times by the chief prosecutor Robert Kempner on the grounds that he was a "possible defendant". Kempner asked Schmitt about his contribution to the "theoretical underpinning of Hitler's Großraum politics" and about his involvement in the preparation of the Nazis' "war of aggression". Schmitt responded that though he might share some "'ideological' responsibility" for the Third Reich, he did not see this as "justiciable" as far as the Nuremberg trials were concerned. In early May his status was downgraded to that of "voluntary witness", and on 13 May he was released (Mehring 2014, pp. 416–419).

Carl Schmitt's vision of politics

Schmitt's method for understanding politics began not with politics as usual, but with those moments when something or someone exercises power in its fullest form. Under normal circumstances power's functioning is restricted by law; it is of course capable of enforcing norms, but only within the confines of norms encoded as law. While law remains in force power will only ever appear diminished. But there are times, "states of exception", when law is suspended and power is able to rise above legal constraints to impose its own norms, autonomous and wholly visible. This is power at its fullest and purest.

States of exception do not occur within the realms of the legal, but nor are they states of disorder; law has not, after all, been erased, but simply put on hold, so a kind of juridical order still keeps chaos at bay. It is precisely this uncertain limbo between the legal and the disordered that allows states of exception to reveal law's operation at its barest (Schmitt 2005, p. 12). Anyone or anything that wishes to establish a norm in a state of exception cannot simply create a law by announcing a norm, because all law is suspended along with the juridical order that would usually ensure its enforcement. Under such extreme circumstances a norm must simply be enforced by whoever or whatever has the power to do so, which involves a decision about *how* practically it should be enforced—over which group of people, and in which way.

Thus states of exception reveal a more general truth about law—a truth that makes it clear that the existence of both states of exception and a power able to govern them are necessary and inevitable. "The purpose of law", Schmitt wrote in an early diary entry, "is the realisation of the norm. The result to be achieved is not law but a condition that corresponds to the norm" (Mehring 2014, p. 45). Realising a norm—producing a reality corresponding to the norm—necessarily requires someone or something to make a decision, because the content of a norm itself can never tell you everything about its application; reality is never as neat as a formulation in words. Under what Schmitt referred to as "a normal situation" (Schmitt 2005, p. 13), the legal system clearly allocates competence for deciding how to apply particular norms to reality across myriad different agencies. Multiple minor points of uncertainty are so thoroughly distributed throughout the system that we may not even notice them—and this is especially true for liberal constitutional states. But abnormal situations can confront the legal system with surprises: unanticipated applications of the law for which the competence to decide has not been designated in advance (p. 10). In these situations there must be some ultimate power that decides how laws are to be applied, or whether they should be

22 *Podemos' encounter with Schmitt*

suspended. When these abnormal situations coalesce into a generally abnormal state of affairs, there must be some ultimate power able to trigger a state of exception and suspend law altogether so that a normal situation can be restored.

"Normal" situations are so important because they provide the "homogeneous medium" that law requires to operate (Schmitt 2005, p. 13). It is not clear what exactly Schmitt means by this, but it is also not too difficult to guess: norms hook onto reality by naming aspects of it—by referring to "citizens", for example. Suppose there is a law that grants all citizens the right to free enterprise. The law is intended to create a "condition that corresponds to the norm" in which everyone has a more or less equal opportunity to gain wealth through their own enterprise; it is this condition, not the letter of the law itself, that really matters. Now suppose that reality alters to become a little more chaotic: a group of people enter the country who are much better-equipped to compete on the free market than its existing citizens; they are better-educated, have strong connections among themselves and have inherited wealth they can draw on. Yet their status as citizens is disputed. In this case we may be faced with a situation where the intention behind the law—the desired "condition that corresponds to the norm"—comes into conflict with its application if it is interpreted in certain ways. If those responsible for applying the law consider these newcomers "citizens" and give them equal opportunity to compete, then they will monopolise the market and leave the existing population destitute. But if they consider them non-citizens and deny them this opportunity, then they still risk accusations that they are ignoring the letter of the law. In such situations, uncertainty about how to apply the law may paralyse the system entirely.

When reality is this fluid, norms will struggle to latch onto it. This is why, for Schmitt, "[t]here exists no norm that is applicable to chaos" (Schmitt 2005, p. 13); reality must already be sufficiently ordered for norms to grip onto its surface. What counts as "sufficiently ordered", though, will always be a matter of opinion—and yet this matter of opinion will have serious consequences. Cleaning up reality so that the distinction between what does and does not count as a "citizen" is clear, for instance, may involve horrific violence if taken to extremes. It will require decisions about who to include in and who to exclude from a community governed by law, about whose lives to preserve and whose to eliminate. Ugly though it may be, the power to re-normalise reality—and to decide both when it is insufficiently normal and when sufficient normality has been restored—is absolutely necessary for the functioning of any legal order in Schmitt's view. Thus, "like every other order, the legal order rests on a decision and not on a norm" (p. 10).

Podemos' encounter with Schmitt 23

This ultimate decision-making power, for Schmitt, is the power of whoever or whatever is sovereign. Clearly, to be properly sovereign—self-governing—a person or persons cannot be subjected to power of this extreme nature wielded by anyone else. Hence Schmitt's famous claim that "sovereign is he who decides on the exception" (Schmitt 2005, p. 5). Sovereign power must enable its holders to suspend the application of law when they deem it necessary, to restore conditions to a state they consider "normal", and to decide when those conditions have reached sufficient normality for law to be reinstated. Each of these decisions involves the exercise of power beyond the law, but all, Schmitt contends, remain within the realm of the juridical because they concern law's application. To anyone accustomed to seeing the legitimate exercise of modern power as principally the work of words and paper, Schmitt holds up an image of legitimate power at its most brutal.

Having bloodied our comfortable conceptions of legitimate power, Schmitt can do the same for politics. If politics has to do with the exercise of sovereign power, which it does, then politics must be defined as the activity concerned with these exceptional decisions taken beyond the law. Schmitt defines politics accordingly as the business of making decisions about the production of the "homogeneous medium" within which law can function; politics is about the very definition of a political community. Political actions and motives are therefore those, and only those, defined by the distinction between friend and enemy—a distinction that "denotes the utmost degree of intensity of a union or separation, of an association or dissociation" (Schmitt 2007a, p. 26), such that the enemy is seen as "existentially something different and alien" (p. 27). Intensity of this degree means that violent conflict between enemies, "the real possibility of physical killing", is always possible (p. 33 and p. 27). Despite war being "neither the aim nor the purpose nor even the very content of politics", it is nonetheless war that—precisely because it invariably lies beneath the surface of any political activity—creates "a specifically political behaviour" (p. 34).

This definition of "the political" allowed Schmitt to defend a view in which politics was not restricted to a single sphere of life—to the activities of parliament and its constituent political parties, for example. Instead, any association or dissociation, whether economic, religious, or ethnic, could become political if it reached such a degree of intensity that war became a real possibility (Schmitt 2007a, p. 38). This meant that properly political entities were not groupings such as political parties; they were those entities able to decide which groups should be treated as potential enemies in war, and which other groups should not be given this treatment (p. 37). Because properly political entities were capable of deciding under which conditions lives could and could not be risked and potentially lost—of deciding "the critical situation"—it was they that were "sovereign" (p. 38)

24 *Podemos' encounter with Schmitt*

In his earlier work, Schmitt maintained that it was for the state to decide the friend/enemy distinctions that would define politics for its people (Schmitt 2007a, p. 30), because it was only the state—not political parties, churches or labour unions—that was ever really prepared to engage in war. States were therefore the only properly political entities (p. 44). In any case, if such decisions were taken by others—political parties, for instance—the result would be an undesirable intensification of antagonisms within countries that would always be at risk of erupting into civil war (p. 32). When friend/enemy distinctions were limited to those decided by the state, violent confrontations would usually be restricted to conflicts between sovereign states under the rule of international law (p. 46). Despite the latent possibility of violence lurking wherever politics was to be found, Schmitt believed that his concept of the political favoured "neither ... war nor militarism, neither imperialism nor pacifism" (p. 33).

Schmitt's definition of politics allowed him to conclude that there was no doctrine more opposed to the political than liberalism. Liberalism's individualism meant that it was antithetical to friend/enemy groupings underpinned by the possibility of war: groups were never the decisive units in which action would take place (Schmitt 2007a, p. 70). In the past, liberalism's "struggle against the power of the state" perhaps had indeed been political. As the doctrine of an "extraordinarily intricate coalition of economy, freedom, technology, ethics and parliamentarism" fighting against "the residues of the absolute state and a feudal aristocracy", liberalism might once have made sense as a political entity (p. 76). But now these enemies had died off, it was no longer accurate to consider liberalism properly political.

Parliamentary politics was an offshoot of liberalism. Parliamentary political parties were not properly political entities, willing to declare war and capable of separating real friends from real enemies. But this was not the sole reason why parliamentary politics was, in Schmitt's view, a spent force; it might after all serve some function that was not strictly "political" but nonetheless important for the maintenance of democracy. Schmitt thought not. Parliaments and their parties were justified by beliefs that belonged to the moribund "intellectual world of liberalism" (Schmitt 1985, p. 8), not that of democracy.

According to liberal doctrine, individuals could take part in disinterested discussions in which people possessed "shared convictions as premises, the willingness to be persuaded, independence of party ties [and] freedom from selfish interests" (Schmitt 1985, p. 5). Parliament's power was justified insofar as it formed the apex of these discussions—insofar as it was "the place in which the particles of reason that are strewn unequally among human beings gather themselves and bring public power under their control" (p. 35). Once these particles of reason had accumulated,

Podemos' encounter with Schmitt 25

"argumentative public discussion" would ensue and partisan opponents would persuade each other "of the truth or justice of an option", clearing the way for government by consensus (pp. 6–7). Truth would emerge from unrestrained competition, harmony from chaos (p. 35). This liberal world view underpinned not just the "metaphysic of the two-party system" (p. 41) in which "great political and economic decisions" resulted from oppositional debate (p. 49). It also grounded the liberal economic faith that mutual good would emerge from competition in the free market (p. 35).

But the liberal world view was, in Schmitt's view, delusional—especially under the conditions of modern mass democracy. Liberal assumptions about the circulation of reason allowed political representatives to shrink back behind closed doors, operating as part of "committees, and increasingly smaller committees" (Schmitt 1985, p. 49). Not only did this mean that representatives receded from those who they were supposed to represent; it also meant that an economic elite had a much greater say in decision-making than anyone else:

> Small and exclusive committees of parties or of party coalitions make their decisions behind closed doors, and what representatives of the big capitalist interest groups agree to in the smallest committees is more important for the fate of millions of people, perhaps, than any political decision
>
> (Schmitt 1985, p. 50)[1]

Parliamentarism, backed up by liberal thought, merely constructed a "façade" (Schmitt 1985, p. 49) of democracy. Real democracy, as Rousseau and Pufendorf had defined it, only existed where governing and governed were identical—where the people were sovereign (pp. 14–15). This meant that real democracy had to be "direct", not only in a "technical sense" but also in a "vital sense"; decisions had to be the "direct expression" of the people's will (p. 17). Any representative of the people must be capable of expressing the people's will without the mediation of additional discussions into which particular interests could interfere. Parliamentary elections could never hope to express the will of the people, because "the people exist only in the sphere of publicity"; when acting in secrecy and isolation—as they do at the ballot box—individuals exist only as themselves, in "the sphere of the private and irresponsible" (p. 16). Democracy should instead operate through some mechanism of public acclamation. Much better to have "dictatorial and Caesaristic" methods capable of producing "the acclamation of the people" than a parliamentary mechanism that undermined the people's ability to govern themselves (p. 17).

26 *Podemos' encounter with Schmitt*

But direct democracy of this kind was only possible where "the people" constituted a singular, homogeneous unit with a single unanimous will capable of direct expression—which in modern "mass democracy" it no longer did. Modern mass democracy has undone this homogeneity by extending political representation to all adults, pretending that a "democracy of mankind" is not just possible but necessary given that everyone is equal (Schmitt 1985, p. 11). Schmitt is unconvinced. True democracy requires "the people" to be homogeneous enough for there to be unanimity, allowing the general will to be expressed directly (p. 13). As Rousseau says, unanimity must ensure that "laws come into existence *sans discussion*"—without the debate that pollutes parliamentary democracy (p. 14). This means that true democracy may require "if the need arises ... elimination or eradication of heterogeneity" (p. 9). One way of doing this is to "exclude one part of those governed"—barbarians, the uncivilised, atheists, aristocrats, counter-revolutionaries, or slaves (p. 9).

But there is another reason why Schmitt is so concerned about the faulty liberal conception of equality. Democracy, in his view, is fundamentally about the equal treatment of equals. If this is to have any substantive meaning, there must be "at least the possibility and the risk of inequality"—it thus cannot be assumed *a priori* that all people are equal simply by virtue of their being humans (Schmitt 1985, p. 9). If a supposedly democratic state views every human being as "equal"—as so-called "mass democracies" do—then its "equal treatment" will inevitably be substantively meaningless because it cannot practically hope to treat *every*one equally; it simply does not have the reach or resources to do so.

We might consider this a special case of Schmitt's general point, mentioned earlier, that reality will inevitably sometimes need to be cleaned up—its chaotic elements removed and the situation normalised—in order for law's application to be effective. To be effective, laws granting equality must extend only to an ordered subset of the global population, not the chaotic entirety of humanity. Schmitt used the fable of "the storks and the frogs" to illustrate his point (Mehring 2014, p. 168). Consider what would happen if both were granted equal rights to seek food with no further intervention. Without providing the storks and frogs with sufficient food to slake all appetites, the former will eat the latter. If storks and frogs are to be considered "equals" within the same political community, then only a weighty investment of resources will ensure equal treatment—and the example could be repeated with alligators added to the allegorical polis. Given finite resources, at some point it will be necessary to tighten the community's borders and exclude some—be they storks or alligators or some other creature—from consideration as equals.

Podemos' encounter with Schmitt 27

The fable of the storks and the frogs shows us how under conditions of formal equality extended to all, real inequalities will not disappear but will simply be ignored since they never enter the sphere of the state as a problem (see Schmitt 1985, p. 12). They will instead be allowed to play out unhindered in the economic sphere. Politics—because it is no longer concerned with equality, substantively understood—will become dominated by antagonism between opposing economic forces, fuelled by persistent inequalities (p. 13); the "storks" will be able to buy influence. The fundamental substantive concern of politics will become that of economic interest, not equality. Democracy's defining feature will have disappeared. This is why "mass democracies" end up in crisis.

Thus Schmitt's cure for democracy's ills is to do away with the institutions of parliamentary democracy and replace them with a form of direct democracy in which the people, a homogeneous group, make decisions through public acclamation—perhaps through dictatorial or Caesaristic mechanisms. Once the people are sovereign, they should be able to take any decision about their own fate, up to and including the most extreme decision about when their life should be risked. Laws and even constitutions can be changed or suspended by the will of the people (Schmitt 1985, p. 15); law does not lie beyond the domain of their sovereignty. Democratic politics must be oriented around decisions about who is among the equals and who is not, and to be properly political, such inclusions and exclusions must take on their most extreme character—they must be decisions about who is friend and who is enemy. Not everyone can be an equal friend, if democracy is to have any substantive meaning; some must be unequal enemies. This is why, for Schmitt, "Bolshevism and Fascism ... are, like all dictatorships, certainly anti liberal but not necessarily antidemocratic" (p. 16).

Schmitt's realist view of politics is barely veiled behind a long summary of Georges Sorel's *Réflexions Sur la Violence* at the end of his essay on parliamentary democracy. In Sorel's philosophy, Schmitt wrote, "Discussing, bargaining, parliamentary proceedings, appear a betrayal of myth and the enormous enthusiasm on which everything depends" (Schmitt 1985, p. 69). Myth and enthusiasm—and in the modern period specifically *national* myth and enthusiasm—were the lubricants without which Schmitt's true direct democracy by acclamation was unable to function. Irrationalism must be substituted for liberal rationalism (p. 76); as in Sorel's philosophy, "[a]gainst the liberal mercantilist image of balance there appears another vision, the warlike image of a bloody, definitive, destructive battle" (p. 69).

Though in Schmitt's earlier work it was the state, as the only entity able to wage war, that must take political decisions about equals and non-equals, he later recognised that in the twentieth century this might no

28 *Podemos' encounter with Schmitt*

longer be the case. As the state became less and less capable of protecting its people from their enemies through war, it could no longer claim to be *the* political entity. Partisan groups without state backing would increasingly take the possibility of war-waging into their own hands (Schmitt 2007b, pp. 11–14). Partisans were not motivated by private gain, but by a desire to fight "at a political front" for the good of a "politically active party or group" (pp. 14–15). They might fight for "revolutionary parties", whose wars had come to replace those of the state since the start of the twentieth century (p. 49). Since they had become the pre-eminent war-waging force of their time, it was these partisan groups, often bound together in revolutionary parties, which now constituted properly political entities capable of distinguishing between friends and enemies (p. 52).

The partisan group carried both the torch of politics and consequently that of democracy into the twentieth century. The first of Schmitt's historical examples of a partisan group is the Spanish guerrilla force that, between 1808 and 1814 "defended the soil of the homeland against a foreign invader", Napoleon (Schmitt 2007a p. 74; Slomp 2005, p. 506n). And yet Schmitt declares that in the Spanish Civil War, just over a century later, "partisans played no significant role" (Schmitt 2007a p. 53). Franco's forces had depended on "assistance from a regular [external] power", Nazi Germany, which for Schmitt was one of the defining characteristics of the partisan (p. 74). Still, on Schmitt's definition the partisan must also be an "irregular fighter" (p. 14)—not part of a "regular state army" (p. 11)—whereas Franco was a general in the state's army, his followers were regular soldiers, and they had presented their military coup against the Republican government in 1936 as a regular defence of the Spanish state against an alien force.

The Republicans also presumably failed to qualify as partisans for exactly the same reason: it was after all the Republican-governed Spanish state that put up resistance to Franco. Both the Republicans and the Nationalists held some state power on their side; this was partly why the conflict had been so protracted. But the resistance that Spanish Republicans continued to put up after Franco's victory, directed by the exiled Partido Comunista de España (PCE —Communist Party of Spain) in the south of France, has all the hallmarks of partisan politics conducted through guerrilla warfare. In 1944, close to the end of the Second World War, they had staged a short-lived invasion of Spain through the Pyrenees. Throughout the remainder of the 1940s the PCE co-ordinated *Agrupaciones Guerrilleras*, guerrilla groups embedded in Spain itself, which continued to put up armed resistance to the Franco regime into the early 1950s. But Schmitt makes no mention of these forces. This was doubtless partly because he first presented the text of his *Theory of the Partisan* in Spain in 1962, at the

Podemos' encounter with Schmitt   29

invitation of Francisco Franco himself. His lectures were held at the Palafox institute, which had been opened at the behest of Franco and was named after the general who led the Spanish resistance against Napoleon. Since Schmitt had reasoned that it was the partisan group that was the true political force of the twentieth century—and since the Francoists seemed to be aligning themselves with Palafox's partisan resistance—it would have been undiplomatic at best to claim that the post-war Republican resistance was a significant partisan group whereas Franco's forces were not.

But there might be another reason why Schmitt neglected to mention the post-war Republican resistance. On his own account, partisan politics could only end in the complete annihilation of the enemy, such was the force of the enmity that animated partisan struggle (Slomp 2005, p. 511). Referring to either antagonist as "partisan" would be to advocate an extension of the civil war and its battles, which the Franco regime was by this point keen to consign to the past, as it sought to open itself up to the rest of the world, economically and politically. Despite seeing the possibility of war beneath all politics, Schmitt did not favour war over peace; recognising the potential for war was nonetheless an essential part of the realist perspective required to assess how peace could be achieved. Schmitt's 1977 call for amnesty in Spain can be understood in this light.

Schmitt's links with the Franco regime went further than the two lectures he gave in 1962. In the 1930s Francisco Javier Conde, who later became one of the foremost intellectuals and politicians under Franco's regime, stayed in Germany and studied with Schmitt, whose books he translated into Spanish. Two of Schmitt's later works were translated into Spanish by his daughter Anima, who had married Spanish professor of philosophy of law and member of Franco's Falange party Alfonso Otero Valera (López García 1996, pp. 142–143). More of Schmitt's books were translated into Spanish, according to Schmitt scholar Jan-Werner Müller, than into any other language (Müller 2003, p. 134).

To Conde, Schmitt's realist conceptual language seemed a good fit for Franco's Spain immediately after the Civil War. This would have been no surprise to Schmitt. As early as 1923 one of his readers, the jurist Richard Thoma, suggested that it was Schmitt's "unexpressed personal conviction ... that an alliance between a nationalistic dictator and the Catholic Church could be the real solution [to the crisis of parliamentary democracy] and achieve a definitive restoration of order, discipline and hierarchy"—although Schmitt rejected this imputation at the time (Kennedy 2004, p. 77). Whatever Schmitt's personal views, Franco's apologists found his work rich in material for legitimising such an alliance. For Conde, Schmitt's antagonistic vision of politics seemed to recognise "the political situation such as it is" rather than as it might ideally be (López García

30 *Podemos' encounter with Schmitt*

1996, p. 143). Schmitt helped writers such as Conde, Eustaquio Galán and Luis Legaz Lacambra articulate the necessity of eliminating the Republican "enemy" politically in order to form a new national Spanish state (pp. 143–144). Through these scholars his ideas had a direct link to the heart of Franco's regime: from 1939 Conde was a member, and from 1949 president, of the Instituto de Estudios Políticos, an "ideological instrument" for Franco's party, the Falange (Müller 2003, p. 134; Sesma Landrin 2004).[2]

Schmitt's thought was also useful for producing a post-hoc justification of Franco's coup against the Republican government in 1936. His elevation of the popular will above law and the constitution legitimated the "rupture" of republican legality produced by both Franco's military uprising and the Civil War that followed (López García 1996, p. 150). Since in Schmitt's view the capacity of constitutional legality to produce order depended on the political decision, scholars such as Luis Legaz Lacambra were able to use Schmitt's thought to criticise Spain's pre-war Republican regime, depicting Franco as the only one capable of taking the decision necessary to produce order (López García 1996, p. 151). Coincidentally, the Weimar constitution that Schmitt originally had in his sights had heavily influenced that of Spain's Second Republic, written in 1931 (Müller 2003, p. 135). Schmitt's arguments about the flaws of liberalism and parliamentarian in Weimar Germany must have resonated particularly strongly with the Francoist intellectuals.

It was also, it seems, through Schmitt that Legaz first came across the thought of Juan Donoso Cortés. Though Donoso had largely been forgotten in Spain by the time of the Civil War, Schmitt frequently referred to his writings. Donoso's *Discurso sobre la Dictadura*, given in the Spanish Cortes on 4 January 1849, defended the lifting of constitutional guarantees by General Narváez. Narváez was responding to fears that the revolutionary fervour that swept Europe in 1848 would travel to Spain (López García 1996, p. 153). "When law is enough to save society, law", Donoso declared; "when it is not enough, dictatorship" (p. 153). On Schmitt's interpretation, Donoso had elevated the political decision above all else, replacing alternative ultimate criteria of legitimacy such as the divine right of monarchs or, indeed, liberal discussion (López García 1996, p. 154; Schmitt 2005, ch. 4).

But while for Schmitt—and, in his view, Donoso—there was nothing beyond the decision to which the decision must appeal, this was not satisfactory for Spanish writers under Franco. They saw in Schmitt's work an absence of any absolute criterion of truth or justice—transcendental truths in which the decision could be grounded. Yet law in the Franco regime must, they maintained, be grounded in *natural* law. Fortunately, Spanish scholars found in Donoso precisely such a grounding, which Schmitt had

Podemos' encounter with Schmitt 31

neglected to adopt alongside Donoso's doctrine of the political decision. That grounding was God. For Donoso, and for the Francoist thinkers, it was insofar as the political decision reflected the will of God that it was legitimate. This helped to justify the Civil War begun by Franco and his troops as a "Sacred War" (López García 1996, p. 155); Franco himself was nothing less than *Caudillo* "por la gracia de Dios" (Müller 2003, p. 136).

The Shadow of Schmitt in Podemos' political thought

Despite their party's success in the 2015–16 Spanish general elections, the Podemos leaders' early rhetoric does not identify lasting dominance in parliament as their ultimate goal. According to Iglesias, Podemos in its guise as a parliamentary party is a "phenomenon of exceptionality" (Iglesias 2015a, p. 166), formed only because Spain's current constitutional regime is undergoing a crisis—"a moment of exceptionality" (p. 158). If the political situation normalises, "Podemos will not play a key role as a political force for winning elections" (p. 166), but will have to adopt other tactics through which to pursue regime change. Parliament is not seen as entirely inimical to democracy, as it is for Schmitt, but nor is it thought essential to democracy's proper functioning; on a tour of Ecuador Iglesias conceded that he thought the European Parliament was "a waste of time", though he has not said the same about the Spanish Cortes (Cid 2015, p. 16). But liberalism, which for Schmitt underpinned parliamentarianism, is less ambiguously condemned as democracy's enemy—though Iglesias and Errejón often target what they call "liberal-conservativism". As a political form in which there is "popular sovereignty" (Errejón and Mouffe 2016, p. 115 and p. 133), democracy requires the possibility of politics. Meanwhile liberalism "incorporates, to some extent, the possibility of cancelling politics, or of having societies which are as empty of politics as possible" (p. 116):

> In the liberal-conservative utopia of a fully reconciled society, in which democracy coincides with absolute consensus, politics is reduced to three or four things that a handful of technicians—no doubt all educated in the same administrations, the same think tanks and the same neighbourhoods—can manage, since what is most fundamental has all already been decided.
>
> (Errejón 2015c)

The old "liberal-conservative" fantasy "flirted with the possibility of the existence of a democracy without the people … a democracy of consumer citizens lacking in collective will" (Errejón 2015c). Neoliberalism has helped this fantasy to become reality, through its "demobilisation and

32 *Podemos' encounter with Schmitt*

pulverisation of social links and of the shared meaning essential for the existence of political community as something more than the sum of its individuals and groups of private power" (Errejón 2011a, p. 2). This fantasy-made-reality has led to a situation where "[P]olitical representatives" have "come to resemble each other more and more, and their constituents less and less ... institutions are increasingly under the sway of powerful minorities" (Errejón and Mouffe 2016, p. 65). Parliament is the place where established "political machines ... operate within the same frame of consensus—which is itself agreed outside the reach of popular sovereignty" (p. 25). There are strong echoes here of Schmitt's words about the Weimar parliament of the 1920s: a small group of committees manage the nation without the direct input of the people, whose voice is restricted to the private, individualised act of regular voting.[3] Even many of those who call themselves progressive are accused of associating "[a]nything that isn't the fragmentation of the isolated citizen and the consumer that takes part in elections" (Errejón 2015c) with totalitarianism. These liberals would rather see "solitary individuals who make decisions dispassionately, and preferably not in the streets but from the comfort of their own sofas" (Errejón and Mouffe 2016, p. 66). But in Podemos' view it is precisely this model of politics that must be overcome through the construction of a new "popular will"—which can only be achieved outside parliament. This is the key to restoring democracy.

Achieving consensus in parliament should not, then, be the primary aim. Instead, Podemos wishes "to defend a vision of the country for the great majority that will be perceived as such"; this is how a new "collective will" can be formed. Doing so will require a large dose of that myth and "enormous enthusiasm" which Schmitt contrasted with the dry conversation favoured by liberals; Podemos' work will consist in "establishing structure and organisation, penetration and territorial rootedness, symbols, songs, names, myths, leaders and programmes" (Errejón and Mouffe 2016, p. 9). Emotion must be "reclaimed" for politics, the "joy of shared collective forms of identification" rediscovered (p. 66). And this, as Errejón says, "is a task that has different stages and rhythms from those of electoral battle" (p. 9).

Uniting fragmented citizens in a new "collective will", however, can only be done if the people have something to unite *against*: the "anti-people" (Errejón and Mouffe 2016, p. 57). In this assumption the Podemos intellectuals side with Schmitt; to sustain the horizontal connection among members of "the people" that democracy requires, others must be excluded. Such equal treatment of equals and unequal treatment of unequals will only "escape politics to go elsewhere" if it is not given political form (p. 62). Parliamentary success is, for Podemos, merely a means to the much

Podemos' encounter with Schmitt 33

more significant end of uniting the people—and this means uniting them against the enemy, against those who should not be considered among the community of equals that is "the people". It is "simply not possible" to "govern for both millionaires at the top of society and for the majority of ordinary people" (Iglesias 2015d, 10:00): a choice must be made, a decision taken.

This became especially clear at the time of the 15-M protests, when those in power lacked the resources to respond to ordinary people's grievances because they had accepted the Troika's austerity programme (Errejón 2015a, p. 20). A choice must be made, and Podemos chooses to include "the people" and exclude the elite of politicians and millionaires, *la casta*. Many members of *la casta* are not true Spaniards: they are people without a homeland. Financial elites with bank accounts in Switzerland or Andorra have no more homeland than do their bank accounts (Iglesias 2014d, 8:00); they are "traitors" (Iglesias 2014c, 2:45). In Iglesias' rhetoric members of this *casta* are even depicted, as Schmitt believed the enemy should be, as "existentially something different and alien" (Schmitt 2007a, pp. 26–27); they are "cats" and the people "mice", preyed on by the elites (Iglesias 2014c, 8:30). The metaphor is taken from a story popularised by Canadian politician Tommy Douglas, which ends with the mice realising that the problem is not the kind of cats they are voting for, but rather the fact that they are cats and not mice (Torreblanca 2015, p. 150). It is the "will to depose the *casta*", the preying cats, that provides the catalyst for the new "collective will" to form (Errejón 2015c).

To expel the elites, "the people" must unite and defend their homeland; "it isn't a political party that's going to change this country", Iglesias declared at one of Podemos' rallies, "it's the people" (Iglesias 2014c, 21:20); "only the people save the people" (22:05). Iglesias charts a national history of the people that begins in the same place as Schmitt's history of the partisan: the day in 1808 when citizens of Madrid repulsed Napoleon's troops (cf. Schmitt 2007b, p. 3). Beginning a speech in Zaragoza, Iglesias remarked that during the war of independence against the French, when faced with the most powerful army in the world, it was women from this city that put up resistance—and that more of this kind of resistance is needed today to bring about political change (Iglesias 2015d, 0:01). But unlike Schmitt, Iglesias continues this history of the popular force he wishes to unite beyond the nineteenth century, citing the Second Republic of the 1930s against which Franco staged his coup, the resistance during the Franco years, and May 2011 when the *indignados* occupied the capital's streets and squares as eruptions of its spirit.

Clothed in this rhetoric, Podemos assumes a shape very similar to that of Schmitt's partisan. Schmitt believed that the partisan emerged under

34 *Podemos' encounter with Schmitt*

circumstances where the state had lost the capacity to wage war against the enemies of its people. The Podemos leaders' early rhetoric suggests that the party's emergence as a political force is justified for similar reasons: it is now Merkel's Germany that is the great enemy of Spain's people, and its allies—the Spanish elites—have done nothing to defend Spain against it. "[D]efending Europe and democracy, today", Iglesias writes, "means all of us, united, confronting German power" (Iglesias 2015a, p. 172). "We [in Southern Europe] don't want to be a colony of Germany, of the financial elites"; this is why the force that Podemos represents must oppose Germany's "financial totalitarianism" with their "democracy" (Iglesias 2015c, 14:08). "[O]ne of the principal problems of democracy in Europe", in Iglesias' view, is "the German government" (Iglesias 2015a, p. 171).

While Podemos does not prescribe war, its leaders' early rhetoric is consistently bellicose. It was through a strategy of "Blitzkrieg" that Podemos initially rose to prominence in the European elections in 2014 (Iglesias 2015a, p. 56 and p. 106 and p. 158; Errejón and Mouffe 2016, p. 150). Its grand aim, to change the "meaning" of everyday reality so as to usher in a new political regime, "is done through a battle, which is fortunately", Errejón seeks to reassure his listeners, "*normally* pacific" (Errejón 2015b, 22:35; our italics). There is frequent talk—consistent, it must be said, with Gramsci's own language—of trench warfare. "[W]e are at the gates of a battle", Iglesias declared before the 2015 elections, "and with few hours to go before we leave the trenches with bayonets, we cannot turn taciturn and think about when we were not at war or when it will end" (Iglesias 2015a, p. 156). After all, it is "a fundamental lesson of history" that "heaven is not taken by consensus, heaven is taken by assault" (Iglesias 2014d, 14:40). This language might be dismissed as just so many metaphors, especially given its Gramscian heritage; surely war does not *actually* lurk as a possibility beneath politics as Podemos understands it. But Errejón makes clear that the passion needed to unite the people in a collective will cannot do without the possibility of violence; it is precisely "the intensity of the clash" from which such passion is derived. As for Schmitt, "[i]t's undesirable, but violence constitutes the ultimate possibility, it is part of the clash" (Errejón and Mouffe 2016, p. 63).

To say, as Luque Sánchez does, that "for Podemos, the history of Spain is basically the history of its wars" may be hyperbolic (Luque Sánchez, 2016). But this history is without doubt deliberately invoked by Podemos' leaders. Iglesias refers to those young people who have been forced by Spain's economic distress to live and work abroad, and who have set up Podemos "Circulos", as "exiliados". Previous groups of exiles in Spain's history, expelled by military force, are brought to mind: those exiled under Napoleon's occupation from 1808–14 and those exiled under Franco's regime (Iglesias 2014d, 5:40). This is a link Iglesias draws explicitly in a speech given in September 2015 in Paris, the city that welcomed many of Spain's exiles from 1939 onwards (Iglesias 2015a, p. 209–10). In a single word, Iglesias manages to associate the current Spanish regime and its Troika-imposed austerity programmes with previous European dictatorships installed through war. Implicitly only a partisan struggle can restore Spain to its own people and welcome the exiles home again.

Once a new collective will has been constructed though a partisan campaign, popular sovereignty can be restored. "The people" rather than the elites will be in power, the rulers identical to the ruled. At that point even Spain's constitution might legitimately be altered or overturned. Of particular significance here are the secessionist movements in Catalonia and the Basque Country, whose demands the current Spanish regime rejects as unconstitutional. For Podemos, by contrast, it is through "a process of popular constitution"—not through the written, legal constitution—that questions such as the degree of "pluri-nationality" and the place of the "right to decide" will be settled (Errejón and Mouffe 2016, p. 149). These are after all decisions about who should be included and who excluded from the political community; they are decisions that pertain to the constitution, but which must, as Schmitt argued, lie beyond the constraints of constitutional law. In Catalonia's case, Podemos' leaders propose a referendum—one in which they will argue for Catalonia to remain within Spain, but whose result may lead to what others see as the unconstitutional secession of the Catalan nation (Iglesias 2015a, p. 124). "A referendum", Iglesias has said, "is always, always, always politically binding"; when the people expresses its collective will, there must be the possibility of a new "constitutional process" (p. 125).

While the Podemos intellectuals' early rhetoric does not directly endorse the "dictatorial and Caesaristic" mechanisms that Schmitt views favourably, their models for a deepened form of democracy—taken from Latin America—suggest they are certainly not hostile to a very strong style of individual leadership. Indeed strong individual leadership may be essential: "it's quite possible", Errejón says, "that there could never be a construction of a general will that didn't crystallise, in one way or other, into some kind of representation involving an affective bond with a charismatic leader" (Errejón and Mouffe 2016, p. 109). There may be a risk of strong leadership giving rise to (and here Errejón distances himself from Schmitt) "decisionism" or "forms ... that can be detrimental to democracy, or to picking the best ideas" (p. 110). But it is a mistake, in Errejón's view, to assume that popular political formations that pivot on affective identification with a strong leader necessarily bring with them "a reactionary danger". The history of Latin American politics has shown that it is

36 *Podemos' encounter with Schmitt*

through this kind of national-popular political organisation that "the experiences of the masses" may be most effectively "included into the state" (p. 92).

First encounters

Much of Schmitt's influence on Podemos' political thought can be inferred from its leaders' statements. But Errejón and Iglesias also make explicit reference to Schmitt. In his article *What is political analysis?*, for example, Errejón claims that Podemos' main task—"the practices of construction and mobilisation of shared sense"—are "always concerned with the constitution of aggregations that follow the pattern friend/enemy, as the political theorist Carl Schmitt points out" (Errejón 2011a, pp. 3–4). His interpretation of Gramsci is, accordingly, a Schmittian one: Gramsci's war of positions is "that activity of articulation which composes the [opposing] camps and mobilises them" through violence, protests or elections. None of these modes, however, precludes conflict as the "ultimate foundation of the alignments" (p. 9). "In Carl Schmitt", Errejón has said elsewhere, "I think there is a positive contribution as long as it is made compatible with pluralism. There can be a logic of adversaries compatible with pluralism" (Errejón and Lassalle 2015).

Though direct references to Schmitt are few and far between, some passages of Errejón's work echo Schmitt's thought so closely that his influence is unmistakable. Consider the following, published two years after Errejón's article *What is political analysis?*:

> Every regime is founded on an exclusion, on a juridical order and a narrative that ban that which is not permitted, that which has no place, that which the order has set itself up against. There is no regime, nor any political subjectivity, without an 'outside'. The management of pluralism is always, for that matter, the management of a frontier: whatever differences have a place inside are minor differences, agonistic and not antagonistic, reason for dispute and not for open warfare; radical differences have no place because they represent threats to the coherence of the edifice, and so are situated beyond the order of the possible, of the respectable and, finally, of the legal.
>
> (Errejón 2013, p. 2)

It was through Chantal Mouffe's writing that Errejón first came across Schmitt, a German wolf wrapped in a Belgian sheep's clothing (Errejón and Mouffe 2016, p. 54). Mouffe agrees with Schmitt's assessment that politics has an ineradicable "antagonistic dimension" (Mouffe 2013, p. 3).

Podemos' encounter with Schmitt 37

So Schmitt is correct to be suspicious of the "rationalist belief in the availability of a universal consensus based on reason" (p. 3); such consensus is often impossible. Yet for Mouffe it *is* possible, through institutional design, to suppress the antagonistic dimension of politics altogether so that only "agonism" remains. In an agonistic relationship adversaries may struggle against each other, often failing to reach consensus, but unlike in an antagonistic relationship they accept each other's legitimacy (p. 7). Agonism is "a we/they relation where the conflicting parties, although acknowledging that there is no rational solution to their conflict, nevertheless recognize the legitimacy of their opponents. They are 'adversaries' not enemies" (Mouffe 2005, p. 20). The left-right distinction in politics provides the framework for agonism, which is why in Mouffe's view "we should resist the call by post-political theorists to think 'beyond left and right'" (p. 6). Politics need not consist in an enmity that demands the other's expulsion from a community.

The puzzling thing about Mouffe's position is that having agreed with Schmitt's definition of politics, she seems then to want to hang on to a version of the political which lacks precisely that which defines it: antagonism. It is not as though Mouffe's solution does away with antagonism altogether anyway, because there is always a chance—quite a high chance, history would suggest—that there will be some who refuse to play the agonistic game, who are excluded for this reason, and who therefore enter into an antagonistic relationship with those within the agonistic fold. Mouffe admits as much (p. 120). For Schmitt, the political relationship would then by definition be the relationship between those within the agonistic fold and those outside it. Those whose interactions were only agonistic would not be properly political entities, since they would not even be capable of the kind of antagonistic decisions that sovereignty demands. For Schmitt, democracy requires that the people are sovereign, which requires antagonism; for Mouffe, "the task of democracy is to transform antagonism into agonism" (p. 20). In adapting Schmitt's concept of the political, Mouffe does away with its most distinctive element.

But Errejón's appropriation of Schmitt is much purer than Mouffe's— and it is partly for this reason that his appropriation requires further explanation. Whereas Mouffe softens Schmitt's friend/enemy vocabulary to fit within a framework of agonistic, rather than antagonistic, politics, Errejón embraces it fully. In conversation with Errejón, Mouffe expressed dismay that the Podemos strategist seemed to approve of passion that might result in violence. "It's undesirable, but violence constitutes the ultimate possibility, it is part of the clash … I think passion always entails the possibility of antagonism", Errejón replied (Errejón and Mouffe 2016, pp. 62–63). Errejón accepts Mouffe's view that agonism is antagonism that has been

38 *Podemos' encounter with Schmitt*

institutionalised but, unlike Mouffe, he does not believe that institutionalisation effects an ontological change of enemies into mere adversaries, nor does he believe that institutionalisation is necessarily a good thing. The left-right distinction that Mouffe sees as absolutely critical to antagonism's transformation into agonism is rejected outright by Podemos, which seeks to reconstruct politics around a distinction between above and below. In doing so it pulls in precisely the opposite direction to Mouffe's proposed left-wing revival, espousing what she identifies elsewhere as right-wing populist discourse "which is replacing the weakened left/right opposition by a new type of we/they constructed around an opposition between 'the people' and 'the establishment'" (Mouffe 2005, p. 70).

Iglesias adopts a similarly pure Schmittian outlook. At the very latest, he will have come across Schmitt's work at the European Graduate School, where he studied under Giorgio Agamben from 2010–11. Agamben's treatment of the "state of exception", published in 2005, contains lengthy discussions of Schmitt, and when references to Schmitt begin to appear in Iglesias' publications they sit alongside references to Agamben (cf. Iglesias 2013a). Iglesias endorses Agamben's version of Schmitt—which he describes as a "hard", "Schmittian", interpretation. He recounts an incident at the European Graduate School at a debate between Agamben and Judith Butler—also a tutor at the School—on Hannah Arendt's book "Eichmann in Jerusalem". When asked by a student what they thought of the death sentence Eichmann was given, both Butler and Agamben "rejected the question and distanced themselves from any decision about punishment". Iglesias suggested to them that political commitment, if it is to be distinguished from mere administration, will sooner or later entail a decision over life itself; was Agamben and Butler's refusal to engage with the previous student's question not incompatible with their professed political commitment? Butler reproached Iglesias for his Schmittian cast of mind. Iglesias responded that, as Mouffe had recognised, it was necessary to rehabilitate Schmitt against Schmitt himself (reclaiming the political theorist but not the national socialist), and that Agamben's work did as much itself (Iglesias 2009, p. 2). In fact Iglesias' Schmitt is much more Agamben's than it is Mouffe's. From Mouffe Iglesias distils the idea that liberalism's political theory is fatally flawed because it denies that antagonism is ineradicable—but this idea is pure Schmitt, and he makes no mention of Mouffe's attempt to blunt antagonism's sharpened edges into agonism (p. 5).

It is Walter Benjamin's treatment of Schmitt—elaborated in the 1920s and 1930s—that Agamben wants to reclaim, because in Benjamin's treatment we find a "countermovement" able "to loosen what has been artificially linked" in Schmitt (Agamben 2005, p. 87). By placing the exception within the realm of the juridical, Schmitt had legitimised violence exercised by the sovereign but not violence of any other kind. Sovereign violence thereby achieved exemption from condemnation that no other violence could secure. Benjamin, by contrast, sought a legitimate place for revolutionary violence against the sovereign state; as he wrote, the state was at risk of becoming an instrument of fascism. So he claimed that Schmitt's attempt to smuggle the state of exception into the realm of the juridical was conceptually illegitimate. If law is suspended in the state of exception, then the state of exception is outside the juridical, and any violence exercised by a sovereign within the state of exception is also beyond the juridical's reach (p. 59). If violence exercised by a sovereign in a state of exception is still considered legitimate even given its extra-juridical nature, then revolutionary violence should be accorded the same status. Benjamin's critique relativises the state of exception's legitimacy, helping us—in Agamben's view—to "interrupt the working of the machine that is leading the West toward global civil war" (p. 87).

Benjamin also alleged that Schmitt's construal of the state of exception as a state of exceptional normlessness was empirically flawed. In fact, by the late 1930s it had become clear that the so-called "states of exception" invoked across Europe had themselves become the norm. As Benjamin wrote:

> The tradition of the oppressed teaches us that the 'state of emergency' in which we live is not the exception but the rule. We must attain to a conception of history that accords with this insight. Then we will clearly see that it is our task to bring about a real state of emergency, and this will improve our position in the struggle against fascism. One reason fascism has a chance is that, in the name of progress, its opponents treat it as a historical norm.—The current amazement that the things we are experiencing are 'still' possible in the twentieth century is not philosophical. This amazement is not the beginning of knowledge—unless it is the knowledge that the view of history which gives rise to it is untenable.
>
> (Benjamin 1996 [1940], p. 392)

A "genuine state of exception" was desirable because it would deliver an explicitly extra-juridical state of normlessness—not one hidden behind the fiction that it was within the juridical—in which revolution against fascism would evidently be permissible. In a genuine state of exception, revolutionary forces would be able to claim sovereignty and restore "normal conditions" in a way that eliminated fascism. Twenty years after his exchange with Benjamin, Schmitt would acknowledge the possibility that revolutionary forces, in the shape of partisan movements, might be properly political entities (Schmitt 2007b).

40 *Podemos' encounter with Schmitt*

For Agamben, too, the "state of exception" has become the rule—a "technique of government rather than an exceptional measure" (Agamben 2005, p. 7). This has been done by replacing "the declaration of the state of exception" with "an unprecedented generalization of the paradigm of security as the normal technique of government" (p. 14). But in Iglesias' rhetoric we see only some evidence of this Benjaminian revision; it is only "at worst" that law "disappears before exceptionality, that is, before politics in a pure state, which is nothing more than the will of the sovereign" (Iglesias 2015a, p. 41). Iglesias does not reference Schmitt here explicitly— perhaps because his book was written for consumption by a non-academic audience with a delicate constitution—but his words are pure Schmitt. "At best", law is "the rationalised political will of the winners" (p. 41); it is still only in exceptional circumstances—such as the government's war against the Basque separatist organisation Euskadi Ta Askatasuna (ETA), that decisions are "based in exceptionality" (p. 36).

Beyond intellectual culture

It is too difficult to say how many of the Schmittian ideas that run through Errejón and Iglesias' early rhetoric can be traced back directly to Schmitt's work itself. The comparisons set out above suggest that at least some of these ideas have been taken directly from Schmitt; but others, while Schmittian in content, may have been drawn predominantly from the work of Gramscians such as Ernesto Laclau, among others. While working out the precise provenance of these ideas in Podemos' rhetoric may be a valuable endeavour, what interests us more is working out how any political cosmology so Schmittian, and with such an obvious if impure link to Schmitt himself, could have come to inform the outlook of a contemporary, progressive, political party. The paradox to be untangled is that of why this bundle of ideas, which taken as a whole constitutes a Schmittian decisionism, has appealed to two young left-wing politicians in the early twenty-first century—both of whom are evidently aware of their political thought's Schmittian cast. To properly account for this we will move beyond the realm of political theory itself in order to look at how this theory has resonated with layers of meaning that are more profoundly infused in Iglesias' and Errejón's world view.

The account that follows is therefore only partial. A complete explanation of why a Schmittian framework resonated with Iglesias and Errejón would undoubtedly have to describe their prior reading in political theory in more detail. It is easy, for example, to find bellicose metaphors in left-wing authors such as Gramsci, as Errejón himself points out (Errejón 2012, p. 129), and to find an antagonistic confrontation with a political enemy

Podemos' encounter with Schmitt 41

("a specific regime of global relations" that they call "Empire") in the work of Michael Hardt and Antonio Negri (2000, pp. 45–46). Having read these left-wing authors espousing certain Schmittian ideas, Iglesias and Errejón might well have been more sympathetic to Schmitt's decisionism. Clearly past readings lay foundations for future readings; one layer of intellectual culture can provide a hospitable environment for another. But remaining on the level of intellectual culture can only ever have quite weak explanatory power. A generation of left-wing students of political science turned politicians will have been raised on the same diet of academic texts in Spain and elsewhere, but their political statements rarely bear such Schmittian traces. To explain why Iglesias and Errejón are exceptions, we need to focus on more deeply-rooted understandings of Spanish politics based in lived experiences that lie beyond the printed page. Over the next three chapters we will see how Podemos' intellectual leadership developed a political world view that hovers on the border between liberal and non-liberal democracy. It is because this world view does not wholly belong to the conceptual domain of liberal democracy that Schmittian ideas managed to permeate it to such an extent.

Notes

1 "Political decision" is used here in Schmitt's specific sense of defining who is friend and who is enemy.
2 Schmitt himself was made an honorary member of the *Instituto de Estudios Políticos* in 1962 when he gave his lectures in Spain (Mehring 2014, p. 490; Rivas 2006).
3 In the article from which these quotes are taken, Íñigo Errejón refers explicitly to Schmitt's book (unavailable in English) *Diálogo sobre el poder y el accesso al poderoso* (Errejón 2015c).

References

Agamben, Giorgio. 2005. *State of Exception*. Translated by Kevin Attell. Chicago, IL: University of Chicago Press.
Benjamin, Walter. 1996 [1940]. *Walter Benjamin: Selected Writings, Volume 4*. Translated by Edmund Jephcott *et al.*. Edited by Howard Eiland and Michael W. Jennings. London: Belknap Press.
Cid, Rafael. 2015. "Podemos #trending topic". In *Hasta luego, Pablo. Once ensayos críticos sobre Podemos*. Edited by Estela Mateo Regueiro. Madrid: Los Libros de la Catarata.
Errejón, Íñigo. 2011a. "¿Qué es el análisis político? Una propuesta desde la teoría del discurso y la hegemonía". *Revista Estudiantil Latinoamericana de Ciencias Sociales*.

42 Podemos' encounter with Schmitt

Errejón, Íñigo. 2012. *La lucha por la hegemonía durante el primer gobierno del MAS en Bolivia (2006–2009): un análisis discursivo*. Doctoral thesis (unpublished). Faculty of Political Sciences and Sociology, Complutense University of Madrid.

Errejón, Íñigo. 2013. "Régimen". In *Lugares comunes: Trece voces sobre la crisis*. pp. 175–196. Edited by Pablo Bustinduy and Jorge Lago. Madrid: Lengua de Trapo.

Errejón, Íñigo. 2015a. "Pateando el tablero: 'El 15M como discurso contrahegemónico' cuatro años después: Entrevista con Íñigo Errejón". *Encrucijadas. Revista Crítica de Ciencias Sociales*, 9. pp. 1–35.

Errejón, Íñigo. 2015b. "Podemos ya ha ganado las próximas elecciones generales en España". Video available at www.youtube.com/watch?v=aGnbl0sRl-E. Last accessed 16 February 2017.

Errejón, Íñigo. 2015c. "Crisis de régimen y hegemonía". *La Circular*, 10 April. Available at http://lacircular.info/crisis-de-regimen-y-hegemonia/. Last accessed 27 February 2018.

Errejón, Íñigo and Chantal Mouffe. 2016. *Podemos: In the Name of the People*. London: Lawrence & Wishart.

Errejón, Íñigo and José María Lassalle. 2015. "Primer debate PP-PODEMOS, cara a cara entre Lasalle-Errejón". *La Vanguardia*, 29 March.

Hardt, Michael and Antonio Negri. 2000. *Empire*. London: Harvard University Press.

Iglesias, Pablo. 2009. "Los muros de Tebas. La política como decisión sobre la vida o Agamben contra Agamben". *Nómadas. Revista Crítica de Ciencias Sociales y Jurídicas*, 24:4.

Iglesias, Pablo. 2013a. *Maquiavelo frente a la gran pantalla: cine y política*. Madrid: Ediciones Akal.

Iglesias, Pablo. 2014c. "Discurso de Pablo Iglesias en Barcelona". Video available at www.youtube.com/watch?v=lvd28BuFAJY. Last accessed 16 February 2017.

Iglesias, Pablo. 2014d. "Discurso de Pablo Iglesias en Vista Alegre". Video available at www.youtube.com/watch?v=aRUp42NjghE. Last accessed 16 February 2017.

Iglesias, Pablo. 2015a. *Una nueva Transición: materiales del año del cambio*. Second Edition. Madrid: Ediciones Akal.

Iglesias, Pablo. 2015c. "Discurso de Pablo Iglesias en la Puerta del Sol". Video available at www.youtube.com/watch?v=oe-bJXZ_KGk. Last accessed 16 February 2017.

Iglesias, Pablo. 2015d. "Discurso de Pablo Iglesias en Zaragoza". Video available at www.youtube.com/watch?v=lvd28BuFAJY. Last accessed 16 February 2017.

Kennedy, Ellen. 2004. *Constitutional Failure: Carl Schmitt in Weimar*. Durham, NC and London: Duke University Press.

López García, José Antonio. 1996. "La presencia de Carl Schmitt en España". *Revista de Estudios Politicos*, 91. pp. 139–168.

Luque Sánchez, Pau. 2016. "Deprisa, Deprisa". *El País: Opinión*. 11 May.

Mehring, Reinhard. 2014. *Carl Schmitt: A Biography*. Translated by Daniel Steuer. Cambridge: Polity Press.

Mouffe, Chantal. 2005. *On the Political*. London: Routledge.

Mouffe, Chantal. 2013. *Agonistics: Thinking the World Politically*. London: Verso.

Müller, Jan-Werner. 2003. *A Dangerous Mind: Carl Schmitt in Post-War European Thought*. New Haven, CT: Yale University Press.

Rivas, Manuel. 2006. "La 'fiesta sagrada' de don Carlos: El homenaje franquista en 1962 al principal jurista del nazismo, Carl Schmitt". *El País*, 2 April.

Schmitt, Carl. 1985. *The Crisis of Parliamentary Democracy*. Translated by Ellen Kennedy. London: The MIT Press.

Schmitt, Carl. 2005. *Political Theology*. Translated by George Schwab. London: University of Chicago Press.

Schmitt, Carl. 2007a. *The Concept of the Political*. Expanded Edition. Translated by George Schwab. London: University of Chicago Press.

Schmitt, Carl. 2007b. *Theory of the Partisan: Intermediate Commentary on the Concept of the Political*. Translated by G. L. Ulmen. New York: Telos Press Publishing.

Sesma Landrin, Nicolás. 2004. "Propaganda en la alta manera e influencia fascista. El Instituto de Estudios Políticos (1939–1943)". *Ayer, 53*. pp. 155–178.

Slomp, Gabriella. 2005. "The Theory of the Partisan: Carl Schmitt's Neglected Legacy". *History of Political Thought*, 16:3. pp. 502–519.

Torreblanca, José Ignacio. 2015. *Asaltar los cielos: Podemos o la política después de la crisis*. Second Edition. Barcelona: Penguin Random House.

3 Divergent presents

Are there objective features of contemporary politics in Spain that can help explain why Iglesias and Errejón turned to Schmittian ideas? If we were trying to account for why Schmitt developed his decisionist framework in the first half of the twentieth century, our first step would probably be to examine the historical context—the events of the time—to see what might have prompted Schmitt to think as he did. In which case it *prima facie* makes sense to assess whether Podemos' leaders are experiencing anything like the same events in contemporary Spain and, if so, to explain their attraction to Schmittian ideas by appeal to this backdrop. Have the events that led Schmitt to produce his distinctive political theory been echoed by events in contemporary Spain? Have the writer, Schmitt, and his readers, Iglesias and Errejón, been influenced by similar experiences that allow the ideas of the former to resonate with the latter?

Iglesias and Errejón have themselves drawn parallels between Schmitt's Germany and contemporary Spain—and they have done so to suggest that present political reality demands a Schmittian style of politics. They imagine, as Schmitt did, that antagonistic political action is particularly suited to their time and their place and share, at least to some degree, Schmitt's solutions to problems they see as not entirely dissimilar to those that Schmitt himself confronted. But on closer inspection, although some similarities emerge between Spain today and Germany in the 1920s, the dissimilarities turn out to be much stronger. Still, we cannot stop at an analysis of the apparently objective political reality in Spain today; we need to ask not just about the nature of objective political reality, but about how Iglesias and Errejón *see* that reality.

Answering this second question requires us to inspect the two lenses through which they look at contemporary Spanish politics: their memory of Spanish history on the one hand, and their vision of its future on the other—both of which are mediated by personal experience. Politicians do not just respond to present reality; they help to produce it—and to do so they latch onto the alternate realities that pre-exist in their imaginings of

Divergent presents 45

past and future. As these imaginings are examined in Chapters 4 and 5, the reasons for Podemos' appropriation of Schmitt's political theory will become clearer. Even if to us contemporary Spain still does not look much like Weimar Germany, when viewed through Iglesias' and Errejón's imaginings—through what we will later call their personal-political narrative—we should at least begin to see how it might take on some of Weimar Germany's characteristics.

Schmitt and the Weimar Republic

The Weimar Republic is rightly remembered as a fragile and volatile period in German history, although it did contain a (middle-)period of relative stability. Both politically and economically, its early years were remarkably unsettled, as political divisions turned violent and extremist groupings—on both the left and the right—threatened to overturn the Government. Particularly significant were far-right groupings such as the Freikorps and the civil guards, which tended to be highly militarised, invariably used violence and sometimes planned assassinations (Rohkrämer 2007, pp. 147ff.). The Government itself struggled to maintain legitimacy in the face of hyperinflation, reparation costs and widespread scepticism towards the supposed virtues of liberal democracy. Conservative forces tended to see the Republic as they saw the Treaty of Versailles: as a foreign import, unjustly imposed on the German people at great cost (Storer 2013, pp. 27–80). Several political parties questioned the Republic's legitimacy, and those that did recognise its validity could not rely on any political tradition of co-operation and concessions to ensure its survival (Bendersky 2014, pp. 64–84).

In comparison with the earlier period, the mid-1920s were undoubtedly less volatile, especially once the currency stabilised and Germany was no longer isolated diplomatically. But the specific economic structure that emerged made it susceptible to oscillations in foreign investment and international markets. This vulnerability goes some way towards explaining why the Great Depression of the late 1920s and early 1930s hit Germany particularly hard, leading to soaring unemployment, increases in taxes and decreases in public-sector salaries (Storer 2013, pp. 81–140).

On the whole, German writers at the time had little sympathy for liberal democracy and even less so for its specific incarnation in the Weimar Republic. This was certainly the case for the large group of literati who, in the aftermath of the defeat in WWI, romanticised about Germany's lost greatness, the need to recover it and the centrality of a charismatic leader who would galvanise people and help to resurrect Germany (Laqueur 1974, pp. 78–109). The atmosphere in universities was similar; few academics were positively inclined towards the Republic. Within and outside

46 *Divergent presents*

the academy, those who were enthusiastic about the Republic and the liberal project were outnumbered by "*Vernunftrepublikaner*" and ardent nationalists. The former did not express any particular warmth towards the Republic but thought it had its merits or usefulness given the current instability and strife (Gay 2001); the latter had strong reservations about the feasibility and desirability of liberalism and the primacy of reason altogether (Bullivant 1985, pp. 47–70; Laqueur 1974, pp. 183–223; Bendersky 2014, pp. 43–63). So it is not an exaggeration to say that Schmitt's political stance—in particular his critique of liberalism—was more or less in sync with the intellectual climate at the time. If some commentators are right that Schmitt's authoritarian leanings and his anxieties about socialism and communism were stronger than his concerns about liberalism (see, for instance, Wolin 1992; McCormick 2009, p. 5), then this fascination with strong leadership and disquiet about the upward march of the left were shared by many of his compatriots at the time. Likewise, his focus on enmity and death fitted the politics of the day, haunted as it was by memories of the war and ridden with conflicts and assassinations. Yet two features made Schmitt's work stand out. Firstly, he rejected constitutional formalism in favour of an approach that situated public law within a broader political setting (Kennedy 2004). Secondly, he managed to integrate an innovative notion of the political with existentialist overtones into a coherent legal and political theory.

Despite their innovative coherence, Schmitt's theoretical reflections changed dramatically during the Weimar Republic and the first couple of years of the Nazi regime. Initially Schmitt, like many legal theorists at the time, kept aloof from the hustle and bustle of contemporary politics, but events gradually drew him in, eventually so much so that he became entangled in the Third Reich. Some commentators read Schmitt's earlier writings in the light of his behaviour in the early to mid-1930s and this is understandable given how far he eventually went to show his support for Hitler. But it is worth bearing in mind that, especially during its earlier years, Schmitt accepted aspects of the Republic and its constitution, albeit reluctantly. Of course, his defence of the Republic was a qualified one and he proposed a distinctive interpretation that celebrated the role of presidential emergency powers, but he was still operating within the contours of liberal democracy. It is important therefore to provide some historical context, however cursory, to make sense of his development.

Schmitt's development

Between 1918 and 1919, when Schmitt was writing his earliest work on politics, Germans lived on the edge of anarchy. As it became clear towards

Divergent presents 47

the end of September 1918 that Germany was losing the war, General Erich Ludendorff, head of the Supreme Army Command, recommended to the Kaiser that the country transition swiftly from a constitutional monarchy to become a parliamentary monarchy so as to appease American President Woodrow Wilson. That way the request to the allies for a ceasefire could come from a democratically-elected government. On 28 October, the Imperial Constitution was amended accordingly to make the Chancellor and his Secretaries of State accountable to the Reichstag and Bundesrat rather than to the Emperor.

Meanwhile, in the northern port cities of Kiel and Wilhelmshaven, word spread that the Imperial Naval Command was planning a final and unauthorised attack against the British Royal Navy. The German sailors mutinied. Led by the mutineers, thousands of sailors, soldiers and workers took control of the cities' governing institutions. Within days several major German cities had come under similar control; Munich, where Schmitt had been working for the deputy general command since 1915, was among them.

Friedrich Ebert, head of the largest party in the Reichstag, the German Social Democrats (SPD), became convinced that the Kaiser's resignation was the only way to avoid all-out revolution. Wilson's diplomatic notes also suggested that the Kaiser's continuing presence would obstruct the negotiation of an armistice. Under pressure from Ebert and his SPD colleagues and with protests mounting in Berlin, Chancellor Prince Maximilian von Baden announced the Kaiser's abdication on 9 November 1918, despite not having secured any such agreement from the Kaiser himself. Ebert then convinced Prince Maximilian to hand the Chancellorship to him, even though constitutionally the power to appoint a Chancellor still lay with the Kaiser alone. To Ebert's consternation his SPD colleague Philipp Scheidemann decided to declare to the crowds assembled outside the Reichstag that Germany was now a Republic. In fact this was not true; the Kaiser had not officially abdicated and the Imperial Constitution still remained in force. Even when the Kaiser finally announced his abdication from exile in the Netherlands on 28 November, the Imperial Constitution remained the only one in force, although it was technically meaningless.

The Kaiser's abdication did not, as Ebert hoped, weaken the revolutionaries' enthusiasm. Over the next few weeks they attempted to transform the Empire into a socialist republic by setting up Workers' and Soldiers' Councils across Germany. They were opposed by both Ebert's SPD and by the German Supreme Army Command—but Ebert was forced first to collaborate if he was to diminish their power. After the revolutionaries occupied the Reichstag and demanded the election of a revolutionary government, Ebert worked to ensure that the SPD was sufficiently well represented in this new government that he would effectively retain

48 *Divergent presents*

control. But he soon became frustrated with the revolutionaries, ordering troops to prevent the first General Convention of Workers' and Soldiers' Councils in Berlin in mid-December. Sixteen people died in the confrontation. A week later sailors from the People's Navy Division—who had been refused their pay by the Commander of Berlin because it was widely thought they were sympathetic to the revolutionaries—occupied the Imperial Chancellery. The next day Ebert ordered the Supreme Command to regain control of the Chancellery but, despite killing around 30 of the sailors, they failed to do so.

At the start of January 1919, hundreds of thousands of demonstrators flooded into the streets at Berlin's heart. Many were armed. After several days of protests, troops acting under Ebert's orders—among whom were the Freikorps, under the command of Gustav Noske—confronted the revolutionaries. 156 people died. Freikorps soldiers beat and killed the leaders of the revolt, Rosa Luxemburg and Karl Liebknecht. But the assault on the revolution in Berlin failed to quell revolutionaries elsewhere in Germany. After Noske ordered the Freikorps to attack the Council Republic of Bremen, resulting in the death of 400 people, armed revolts broke out across the country. Workers went on strike in their masses, and fighting broke out in the streets of Berlin. The response of Ebert's government was decisive: Noske ordered the Freikorps back into Berlin where, by mid-March, they had put an end to the unrest at the cost of 1,200 lives.

In April 1919 a Bavarian Soviet Republic was proclaimed in Munich. Five months earlier socialist and anarchist groups had staged a revolutionary coup under the leadership of former journalist Kurt Eisner. After the Bavarian King Ludwig III fled to Austria, Eisner became prime minister of what he declared to be the "free state" of Bavaria. But after regional elections showed comparatively weak support for his parliamentary group among the Bavarian electorate, he was assassinated in February 1919 by the anti-semitic German nationalist Count von Arco auf Valley. In mid-March the Bavarian parliament elected SPD member Johannes Hoffmann as head of an interim minority government, but after he failed to gain adequate support in Parliament the Soviets declared Bavaria a Soviet Republic. Less than a week later, the fledgling Republic was taken over by Russian Communist Soviets, led by a trio of Russians and supported by Lenin's government. The Communists established their own "Red Army" and used it to seize money from private safes and safety deposit boxes, to close schools and newspaper offices and to burn police files. As disorder spread, the Communists took control of all Munich's food supplies and the Red Army looted homes and businesses across the city (Gaab 2006, pp. 58–59). Russian soldiers were brought in to execute twenty "bourgeois" hostages. After a month of chaos, Hoffmann's exiled government asked Berlin for

Divergent presents 49

help and around thirty thousand Freikorps and nine thousand members of the German army converged on the city, killing 1,000 supporters of the Communist government in street fighting and executing a further 700 after their arrest; the Soviet Republic had taken hostage and murdered ten Freikorps men (Hoelzl and Ward 2014, p. xvi). Among the Freikorps troops was the powerful unit led by Hermann Ehrhardt, the eponymous Marinebrigade Ehrhardt, which would go on to play an important role in destabilising the Weimar Government.

Amid what might well have seemed like the beginnings of a civil war, elections were held on 19 January 1919 for what was to become the Weimar National Assembly. Even though Ebert had tried unsuccessfully to prevent the Convention of Workers' and Soldiers' Councils from meeting in December, in the end the Convention had been dominated by SPD followers anyway. Those who attended the Convention voted not to draw up a new constitution based on a council system, but rather to arrange elections for a Constituent National Assembly, as Ebert's government desired. 83% of the enfranchised population, which for the first time included women, turned out to vote. Ebert's SPD became the largest party in the Assembly, entering into a governing coalition with the Centre Party and the German Democratic Party, and Ebert was elected president on 11 February.

Having put down the threat from the far left, the stability of Ebert's Government was challenged from the right just over a year later. Triggered by Gustav Noske's attempt to dissolve it, and at the instigation of the highest ranking general in the German army, Walther von Lüttwitz, the Marinebrigade Ehrhardt occupied central Berlin on 12 March 1920. Erhardt's troops were joined by Wolfgang Kapp—a member of the German National People's Party who had been planning a coup for some time—Waldemar Pabst (under whose command Luxemburg and Liebknecht were killed), Ludendorff, and Lüttwitz himself, together with a battalion of the regular army. Kapp announced that he, not Ebert, was now Chancellor. By this time Ebert's government had fled to Dresden and then Stuttgart, where they called for a general strike to bring down Kapp's coup. The strike, which may have involved as many as twelve million workers, brought Germany to a standstill and left Kapp unable to govern.

Kapp eventually agreed to resign, but at a price: on behalf of the National Assembly, the centre-right parties agreed to new elections and an amnesty for the perpetrators of the coup. Ehrhardt was given assurances that he would not be arrested as long as he and his Marinebrigade left Berlin—which they did, but only after machine-gunning to death twelve civilians who heckled them as they departed. Outside Berlin, meanwhile, the general strike had broken out into a violent struggle between workers and the military. By the end of March, armed workers had taken control

50 *Divergent presents*

over the cities of the Ruhr. After the Government tried and failed to negotiate an end to the workers' revolt, the Marinebrigade joined the army in a bloody campaign to oust them. Hundreds were killed. In the June 1920 elections that followed, support for the SPD fell dramatically, while support rose for the extreme-right German People's Party and the extreme-left Independent Social Democratic Party (USPD).

It was during this tumultuous period, much of which Schmitt spent working in Munich, that his book *Dictatorship* (2013) was written. Schmitt was repelled by the coup and by the atrocities committed by the radicals; this significantly affected his thinking about politics, and his concerns found their way into *Dictatorship* (Bendersky 2014, pp. 21ff.). Back in 1915 Schmitt's superiors had given him the task of writing a "report on the law of the state of siege". The report was to justify the continuation of the state of siege "for several years after the war". Though Schmitt bemoaned his being chosen for this task, and did not like the idea that dictatorial powers might be extended, he also thought his own position unrealistic. Now the politics of post-war Munich had confirmed this view; in the face of apparently irrepressible militarism it was vital to fall back on some mechanism that could preserve the legal order. Dictatorship, the use of emergency powers by an executive authority, was inevitable (Bendersky 2014, pp. 21–40).

A few years later, in an article written in 1926, Schmitt clarified his notion of dictatorship: it refers to any state power that is freed from legal restrictions in order to deal with exceptional situations such as war or rebellion. He famously went on to distinguish between "commissary" and "sovereign" dictatorship; whereas the former operates within the limitations of the constitution, the latter implies an entirely new order (Schmitt 1926; also Hoelzl and Ward 2014, p. xxiv). In Schmitt's view the Communists' ambitions, as events in Munich had revealed, were to replicate the sovereign dictatorship of the Jacobins in revolutionary France (see also Mehring 2014, pp. 104–105). Even more worrying was the prospect that the new German constitution might leave room for sovereign rather than commissary dictatorship.

Between the workers' revolution and the Kapp Putsch, at the end of July 1919, the National Assembly had managed to pass the Weimar Constitution. Article 48 stipulated that under some circumstances the President could issue an emergency decree, and it was to this article that Schmitt attached his critical attention. Since Article 48 suggested that the President could act in a way that was unlimited by law, it implied that he might be able to change and make law unilaterally—that he might assume the role of sovereign dictator (Bendersky 2014, pp. 33ff.). With politics as volatile as it had proved to be, such a provision left the new Weimar state open, at least in principle, to the dictatorship of the proletariat. It was a sign of the Weimar legislature's bourgeois naivety that its members appeared to believe otherwise.

Divergent presents 51

The period Schmitt spent in Munich underlay his subsequent interest in what he called a "counter-revolutionary philosophy of the state", which settled on commissary dictatorship as the only viable system of government in a mass democracy such as 1920s Germany (Mehring 2014, p. 127). Schmitt's *Political Theology* (2006), published in 1922, ended with a history of this philosophy's development; its pivotal point was Juan Donoso Cortés' defence of dictatorship as the only bulwark against the 1848 revolutions. Schmitt's readership must have been struck by the similarities between this historical depiction and contemporary events in Germany. It must have been obvious to the informed reader at the time that the book was making a case for some form of dictatorship (see also Mehring 2014, pp. 127). At this stage, Schmitt was concerned about threats to the state's stability from both left and right, including from the National Socialists. But in the first half of 1923 his views began to change. He met with his former supervisor at the deputy general command in Munich, Captain Christian Roth, who was now working to set up alliances for the National Socialists. Impressed by "the legal-mindedness of the [National Socialist] Bavarian civil servants", and persuaded that the civil service could provide the stability needed by the state, Schmitt became convinced that, by re-establishing state authority, the nationalists could provide the necessary antidote to parliament's failure to form a government (Mehring 2014, p. 136).

In 1923 France and Belgium occupied the Ruhr region, triggering an economic crisis that rendered the Reichstag unable to form a stable government. Rhineland separatists, supported by France, declared a "Rheinische Republik" in Aachen. Adolf Hitler, who had risen to the top of the National Socialist German Workers' Party, made his first failed attempt to seize power in the Munich Beer Hall Putsch. He was supported by, among others, Schmitt's former supervisor, Christian Roth (Mehring 2014, p. 136)—though all the evidence indicates that at that point Schmitt found Hitler and what he stood for abhorrent. Amid the Weimar Republic's continuing disarray Schmitt, now teaching in Bonn, was writing *The Crisis of Parliamentary Democracy* (1988). Political stability, Schmitt suggested, required homogeneity; the liberal belief that the confrontation of radically different perspectives in the public sphere might result in stable democratic government was hopelessly flawed. Instead, a "new form of authority" should be sought—one that might, he implied, look towards the Italian Fascists and their "national myth" for inspiration. Mussolini had become Prime Minister of Italy in 1922. He and his party promised "an authority based on the new feeling for order, discipline, and hierarchy" (Mehring 2014, p. 140). In 1925 Schmitt would claim that Mussolini's assassination was "the greatest disaster conceivable within the realm of politics" (p. 171).

52   Divergent presents

Schmitt's 1927 book *The Concept of the Political* (2007a) defends a vision of the state and its corresponding people as a single, homogeneous political entity whose battle should be not within but without. Germany had suffered the humiliation of military occupation in the Ruhr and the Rhineland, where the French had gone as far as backing secessionists; Russia had backed a Bolshevik coup in Munich. To be worthy of the label, politics should consist in pushing back against these threats, with military force if necessary. By comparison the so-called "politics" of Weimar Germany's politicians tied itself up in trivialities, failing to address the internal heterogeneity that left Germany seriously vulnerable. Schmitt's initial support for the Weimar political order had been gravely damaged. In 1924 he had argued that the Constitution gave the President of the Reich the power to dissolve the Reichstag in case parliamentarism failed; now, after Germany had asked to join the League of Nations in early 1926, Schmitt began to consider failure endemic to parliamentarism—though he would continue to defend the Constitution (Bendersky 2014, pp. 85–103). Membership of the League of Nations threatened to preserve the status quo established by the Treaty of Versailles which, in Schmitt's view, deprived Germany of its rights. The prospect of the "legalization of an unbearable condition between war and peace" would drive Schmitt's work from now on (Mehring 2014, pp. 167–169).

Though the liberalism of the Weimar Republic had failed, democracy could be preserved. An effective form of "direct democracy", he claimed in a Berlin lecture on "Referenda and Petitions for Referenda", could be used in a "process of popular legislature" (an "exceptional process of legislature") that bypassed parliament. The people would be posed a simple question to which they could answer "yes" or "no". Yet this form of direct democracy could only ever work as an exceptional process; if it were to become the sole mechanism by which legislation was produced, there would either have to be "pure" direct democracy—which was an anarchistic utopia—or a fully formalised system—which would be inadequate since the people would lose "their vital greatness and force" (see Mehring 2014, p. 175). Voting is, after all, a private process that interrupts a people's coming together in public. In place of the Weimar regime, Schmitt had begun to advocate an authoritarian system whose democracy was guaranteed not by parliamentarianism but by acclamation, which might occasionally take the form of referenda.

At this stage Schmitt was still defending the Weimar Constitution against what he saw as the mistaken granting of ordinary legislative powers to the President of the Reich. The President should only have the power to make law under exceptional circumstances—if necessary legitimated by a plebiscite; otherwise the Constitution should be upheld. The Constitution, as

Divergent presents 53

he said in an address to the Langnam Association of industrialists in 1930, "is better left in peace, if one does not want to embark on unpredictable and dangerous experiments" (Mehring 2014, p. 233). But in October 1931, Schmitt wrote in his diary that he had "bought national socialist literature" (p. 244). Over the past few years his anti-Semitism had hardened and he had become embedded in right-wing political society. He had also become a supporter of rule by presidential decree, based on the observation that the Weimar Constitution had been progressively undermined (Bendersky 2014, pp. 85–191). Now he considered that the Constitution had been fatally flawed from the outset: it was not one but two constitutions, which undermined each other by admitting a paralysing pluralism into the state apparatus (Kennedy 2004, p. 22; Cumin 2005, pp. 93–134). The only way to save the German constitutional order was to reject that part of the Constitution which gave parliament legislative authority. If this could not be done, then the Constitution should be abandoned (Mehring 2014, p. 257). Though Schmitt at first opposed Hitler's seizure of power, supporting the authoritarian presidents Franz von Papen and Kurt von Schleicher as far as he could in their rule by presidential decree, he came to acknowledge that Hitler's Enabling Act might usher in the renewal of law he had come to believe was necessary (cf. Kennedy 2004, pp. 16–17). At an invited lecture in Weimar in March 1933, he pronounced the death of the Weimar Constitution (Mehring 2014, pp. 271–278). By the beginning of May he had become a member of the National Socialist party, and in July he was appointed a Prussian state counsellor by Hermann Göring (Kennedy 2004, p. 18; Bendersky 2014, pp. 204–205). There then followed a brief period during which Schmitt became intensely implicated in the workings of the Nazi regime (he developed the theoretical outline of the Third Reich and publicly condoned the purges that took place early on, and his speeches became overtly anti-Semitic) until he himself became the target of critics within the National Socialist party. These critics accused him of being a conservative and a crafty opportunist—not a genuine believer in the new Nazi creed. Interestingly, this accusation was aided by the distribution in Germany of anti-Schmittian articles by former friends of his who had been forced to flee abroad, who were appalled by the change in his stance and who pointed out his former association with Jewish and liberal-minded intellectuals (Bendersky 2014, pp. 219–242; Cumin 2005, pp. 143–154).

A Spanish Weimar?

In the decade that followed the end of the First World War, when Schmitt's major works began to appear, Germans lived with violence and militarisation of a kind that most of Europe has not experienced since

54 *Divergent presents*

1945. Men who had fought in the war carried with them the experience and, just as importantly, the weaponry that made multiple armed confrontations possible in many of Germany's biggest cities. Far from ending with the war in 1918, militarisation in Germany continued throughout the 1920s, not least in the form of France and Belgium's occupation of the Ruhr and Rhineland. If Schmitt stressed that politics necessarily risked the most extreme violence, this was because the pen he wrote with was shaken by the rattle of gunfire.

Meanwhile the political instability of the Weimar Republic reached a level of volatility that no European government has come close to experiencing in recent decades. After Ebert was forced early on into exile by the Kapp Putsch, the Weimar Government suffered multiple crises in the early 1920s, and at one point the SDP walked out of the governing coalition. If Schmitt stressed the futility of parliamentary debate, this was because at times the Weimar Government, challenged by extremists, was barely able to hold onto power.

And if Schmitt dwelt on the sinister topic of the need for a "homogeneous" people, this was at least in part because of anti-Semitism and xenophobia nourished by the period's extreme politics. Schmitt had been in Munich when Russian Jews staged their bloody dictatorship of the proletariat, as had the young Adolf Hitler. The spirit of the First World War, in which different nationalities suffered catastrophic losses at each other's hands, was perpetuated—albeit in weaker form—by the Treaty of Versailles and the actions of the French military. With militarised political divisions already falling along ethnic and linguistic lines, heterogeneity was an easy target for a theorist concerned above all with political stability.

Contemporary Spanish politics is not obviously characterised by any of these conditions—at least not strongly so. The executive has for the most part been highly stable since 1978. Although no government could be formed for almost a year after national elections in 2016, Mariano Rajoy remained in charge of a caretaker government as stipulated by the constitution. This relative political stability has been accompanied by minimal militarisation. The long armed conflict with the Basque separatists Euskadi Ta Askatasuna (ETA) took place on nothing like the scale of the conflicts that pervaded the early years of the Weimar Republic. Apart from this, political divisions along ethnic and linguistic lines—such as those between Catalonia and the rest of Spain—have only recently deepened to the point where force has been used, and even at their nadir during the 2017 Catalan independence referendum resulted in very little bloodshed (Rodríguez and Congostrina 2017).

Yet we find Pablo Iglesias writing in 2015 about a real danger that we will soon see "the face of Europe that we know from the times that began

Divergent presents 55

with the Weimar Republic in Germany" (Iglesias 2015a, p. 110), and that Podemos is the bulwark against this. Podemos' Schmittian take on politics is necessary, in his and Errejón's view, *precisely* because the political and economic conditions in contemporary Europe are so similar to those of the 1920s; without giving these conditions the recognition that Schmitt's thought gives them, they will be exploited opportunistically by regressive powers. In such circumstances, abandoning "all forms of collective affects" as well as "national identification" will merely give "the most reactionary forces" the upper hand (Errejón and Mouffe 2016, p. 68). The existence of Podemos ensures that it is not a Schmittianism of the reactionary kind that, as in Weimar Germany, gains the upper hand, but rather a progressive Schmittianism (cf. Iglesias 2015a, p. 54). By appropriating not just Schmitt's language but also some of his preferred political solutions, Podemos' leaders actually see themselves as neutralising Schmittian ideas in the hands of others.

There was in fact a progressive Schmittianism during the Weimar Republic itself, represented by some of the most prominent juridical theorists of social-democratic syndicalism at the time, Otto Kirchheimer and Franz Leopold Neumann. Kirchheimer and Neumann mixed Schmittian theory with Marxism, opposing labour to capital as friend to enemy. Theirs was a Schmittian view of politics transposed to the left, resulting from a similar analysis of the inadequacies of the Weimar regime. But once Schmitt began to support the National Socialists, the progressive Schmittians distanced themselves from him, demanding that the democratic process take place within formal legal constraints (López García 1996, p. 166).

The Germany in which Kirchheimer and Neumann took up Schmitt's work was one held together by what many, including Schmitt, saw as a fragile political settlement. Parliamentary democracy had only recently been established—with Friedrich Ebert's signing of the Weimar Constitution in 1919—following what was effectively a military dictatorship led by Generals Paul von Hindenburg (who was President of the Reich from 1925–1934) and Ludendorff. In the 1920s and early 1930s, when Schmitt wrote what are now his best-known works, the Weimar Constitution could still quite easily be seen as a contingent phenomenon rather than as a necessary part of Germany's political existence—as something that the sovereign people could overturn at will if, as Schmitt came to believe, it was inherently flawed (cf. Schmitt 2007a, p. 15).

The ink of Spain's 1978 Constitution is not quite as fresh today as Weimar Germany's was in the 1920s. Nonetheless, it is only as old as Pablo Iglesias himself. Unsurprisingly, then, Iglesias—whose first degree is in law—found it easy to state in 2014 that "[a]nyone who has studied law knows that constitutions are the rationalised will of the winners or the

56 *Divergent presents*

expression of a relation of forces between different powers" (Iglesias 2014a, p. 151). Compounding this sense of fragility is the fact that the constitution of the Second Spanish Republic, which came into force in 1931, exists in memory as an alternative to that of 1978—at least for those who see its destruction by Franco in 1939 as illegitimate. This is why Zapatero's government could be accused in 2005 of "attempting to establish democratic legitimacy in 1931, not in 1978" (Anson 2005). Conscious of Spanish history, Iglesias takes the view that constitutions themselves are political through and through; as such, they are within the realm of the political, not beyond it. Just as many saw the democracy ushered in by Germany's 1919 constitution as inherently flawed, Errejón considers the democracy that "came into existence during the Transition in the Moncloa Pacts, and later in the Constitutional Pact of 1978" as "weak, timid" (Errejón and Mouffe 2016, p. 26).

The first major impediment to the Weimar Government's proper functioning was, of course, the reparations Germany was forced to pay by the Versailles treaties. Imposed by a union of allied powers, the reparations caused resentment among ordinary Germans, even if ultimately their government managed to pay back very little of what they owed. Thanks to the demilitarisation demanded by the Versailles settlement, the German residents of the Rhineland had become, in Schmitt's view, "an atrocious sort of hostage" (Muller 1991, p. 708), and the German *Volk* dependent on the grace of external powers for its dignity and its survival. There was even a supra-national institution that secured Germany's indignity and dependency, the League of Nations, which Schmitt accused of using the universalistic language of economic liberalism to cover up Germany's subjugation (Muller 1991, p. 708; Kennedy 2004, pp. 109–110). In Schmitt's view the League was a vehicle for the allied powers' pursuit of politics in its proper sense; far from being interested in genuine equality among nations, the allied powers were advancing their own economic imperialism at the expense of the German people. To Schmitt this was inevitable: real politics would always be like this, and to believe otherwise was hopelessly—dangerously—romantic. That the politicians of the Weimar Republic accepted the League's rhetoric rather than responding in kind was further evidence of the ineptitude of liberal parliamentarism.

Ironically it is now Germany that is viewed by some in contemporary Spain as the allied powers were in Weimar Germany. "Europe", specifically the European Union (EU), has taken on the role of the League of Nations. "Europe is actually talked about in Spain", Jorge Moruno writes, "but as if it were something of an external actor, embodied by Angela Merkel, the Troika and the suffering caused by the austerity measures" (Marsili and Moruno 2016). Even before the financial crisis, German-imposed

Divergent presents 57

economic discipline had, in the Podemos leaders' view, weakened Spain's self-sufficiency; the country had been forced to accept a "European division of labour and a sharing of power clearly favourable to German power", in which its development was "based on real-estate bubbles and corrupt urban projects" (Iglesias 2015a, p. 170; Errejón 2012, p. 150). The state privatised more and more of its activities to bring the public debt and its budget in line with EU targets. As private debt rose as a result, creditors in Germany and France became rich (Errejón 2012, p. 151). The Spanish had become hostages within Europe; their welfare state was no longer "dependent on the state's capacity for tax collection", but rather "largely based on European funds". The cause? A Germany that "uses the European Union to impose its revision of the classical neoliberal programme" on other countries (p. 154).

As this story has it, post-2007 Spain has been forced by a union of external powers, the Troika (comprised of the European Commission, the European Central Bank (ECB) and the International Monetary Fund) with Germany at its head, to cut its deficit by imposing austerity policies. As a result, "tens of thousands have been evicted from their homes and the dismantling and privatisation of public-health and education systems has sharply accelerated" as debt has been transferred from private banks to the ordinary people (Iglesias 2015a, p. 170). Just as the terms of the Versailles treaties seemed unjust to many Germans, the terms imposed by the Troika appear unfair to many Spanish people. Iglesias has complained repeatedly that the Troika's austerity policies "humiliate" his country (Torreblanca 2015, p. 154). Unlike France, which avoids sanctions for failing to meet its deficit targets "because it's France"—in the words of the President of the European Commission, Jean-Claude Juncker—Spain has been forced to toe the line (Doncel 2016). "It's difficult to ignore the fact", wrote *El País* journalist Luis Doncel in July 2016, "that not all countries receive the same treatment in the EU, but no European leader had expressed it so bluntly" (Doncel 2016).

During the 2016 elections Podemos' proposed solution to this predicament was first to strip back the EU's rhetoric of equality among its members, revealing Germany's economic neo-imperialism for what it is, and then to renegotiate the terms of the Stability and Growth Pact (SGP) agreed between members of the EU. It would eliminate the SGP's rigid common rules that are justified by disingenuous appeals to treat equals equally. Debt and deficit targets would be tailored to the needs of each individual country, not pegged to suit Germany, and a "mechanism for transferring resources between countries depending on their position in the [economic] cycle" established. In future, the ECB would be statutorily obliged to maintain an "adequate level of economic activity" and to

58 *Divergent presents*

promote job creation—historically a problem in Southern Europe, though not in the north (Unidos Podemos 2016). There is a deep ambivalence here towards the EU (see della Porta, Kouki and Fernández 2017). Europe's union under common institutions *per se* is not the problem for Podemos—indeed it can be a force for good—but as long as these institutions function as a smokescreen for the perpetuation of inequality among Europe's nations, the EU will be profoundly flawed.

It was more than just the Weimar Government's acceptance of the Versailles settlement, however, that reduced its legitimacy in the eyes of Schmitt and other Germans—including Kirchheimer and Neumann. In Schmitt's view, the Weimar Government presided over a subordination of cultural and spiritual life to the economic logic of production and consumption. This has led to an atomistic society in which the individual becomes his or her sole reference point. Against this, Schmitt called for the re-establishment of a broader societal vision that would galvanise people and bring them together (Muller 1991, pp. 704–705).

It is possible to tell a similar story about Spain's recent history. Contemporary Spain has, according to this narrative, seen a similarly fragmenting economisation that has benefited the wealthiest to the detriment of the poorest in society. Economics has been elevated to the highest levels, even to the point at which a 2011 constitutional reform presided over by the Partido Popular (PP—People's Party) and the Partido Socialista Obrero Español (PSOE—Spanish Socialist Workers' Party) "constitutionalised" the balancing of budgets of all Spanish administrations—"nothing other", in Iglesias' view, "than the formalisation of the victory of Hayekian Europe" (Iglesias 2014a, pp. 151–152). With this development, the state's "already extremely limited capacity to exercise sovereignty" has been curtailed, as it has been forced to sacrifice social spending in favour of narrow economic goals (1p. 152). No alternative to the democracy of "isolated" citizen-consumers, "lacking in collective will", feared by Errejón has been permitted (Errejón 2015c; cf. Iglesias 2014a, p. 152). Errejón's solution is redolent of Schmitt's: "Affective involvement as an engine of mobilisation has been key to us: the recovery of the joy of being together, the solidarity between strangers—so present in our rallies and events—the belief in victory and its fearless affirmation" (Errejón and Mouffe 2016, p. 61).

When Podemos' leaders look at Spain today, then, they see a country that is *already* similar in significant respects to Germany in the 1920s—and they have proposed Schmittian solutions to what they identify as the deficiencies of Spanish politics. But it is difficult to fully understand this point of view by taking the facts about contemporary Spain and placing them alongside those we know about Schmitt's Germany. Because of course what is and what is not fact remains profoundly contested. Intellectuals

Divergent presents 59

associated with Spain's centre-left and centre-right parties, the PSOE and PP, offer a very different interpretation of recent events.

Far from being a German imposition, writes sociologist and former PSOE Minister of Education José María Maravall, Spain's harsh route out of the economic crisis was chosen by the governing PP—and the party could have chosen otherwise. It was Mariano Rajoy himself who spun the lie that "the Spanish cannot choose ... We do not have this freedom ..." before Parliament, to which former PSOE leader and prime minister Felipe González retorted that "if he says that he has no freedom to choose he means that in electing him citizens have performed a useless exercise" (quoted in Maravall 2013a, p. 169). From the perspective of a seasoned Spanish politician whose career has been structured by the traditional two-party logic, the existing political elite is obviously not made up of a homogenous cast of neoliberal automatons who all obediently sing to the tune of the international markets. Yes, European economic institutions have been poorly designed, rendering them unable to absorb exogenous shocks, but this is the result more of incompetence than villainy, and has been recognised as such by part of the Spanish political elite, González among them (Maravall 2016, p. 109).

Nor can the country's economisation and its attendant rising inequality be blamed on any conditions endemic to the current system; they result from irresponsible policymaking. After the Socialists won the 1982 elections, there ensued "14 years of social-democratic government in Spain" (Maravall 2016, p. 15). González, who was prime minister at the time, was explicit about his intention to reduce inequality—though since he was interested in the distribution of well-being rather than the "distribution of poverty" he also made clear that doing so would require "economic efficiency" (Maravall 2013a, p. 151). Even if inequality began to rise again in the 1990s, it decreased under the PSOE government in the 1980s (Maravall 2016, p. 97).

And if Spain's population has broken up into a multitude of atomised citizen-consumers, this is because the main political parties have steadily dismantled the connections between politicians and people—not because the 1978 Constitution encourages such apolitical fragmentation. In fact, the 1978 Constitution actually stipulates that political parties' "internal structure and functioning must be democratic", and to begin with, Maravall believes, it was. Until the 1990s, that is—implicitly after the Government he was a member of left office—when things started going downhill (Maravall 2013b; Maravall 2013a, pp. 52–53). Parties began to base their organisation on "bureaucratic principles", investing less and less in activism and entering into geographically-specific alliances with other parties for electoral gain. This has made it very difficult for them to build up a broad and enduring base of support (Maravall 2013a, pp. 53–54).

60 *Divergent presents*

Meanwhile José María Lassalle, a writer, academic, member of the centre-right PP and current Secretary of State for the Information Society and the Spanish Digital Agenda, agrees that the "economicism of the neoliberal model" has caused widespread psychological damage by creating a society saturated with the quantification of consumerism (Lassalle 2017, 672–76/1008). Democratic citizenship was indeed turned into a "basically consumerist" experience (311/1008). But this has been the case across the West, and results from the dominance of neoliberal ideology in the 1990s, not from Spain's particular institutional arrangements (311/1008). It is not just economicism that is to blame, either; it is also our captivation by screens that isolate us in our own individual digital cages (681–87/1008), resulting in "the digital transformation of the person" (692/1008). If affective identification with our fellow citizens is deteriorating, then this is due to one of the main tools through which populism engages with its supporters (753–59/1008). Life lived through screens denies us the experience most likely to prompt us to empathise with others, to *feel* with them: the experience of the body (833–855/1008). It is this experience that liberalism—with its prohibition of torture and illegal detention, its freedom of thought and movement, its concern with the eradication of violence—depends on (844/1008).

It is almost needless to say that Lassalle and Maravall—Iglesias' seniors by 12 and 36 years respectively—both see the 1978 Constitution as a far more robust guarantor of democracy than do Podemos' leaders. When Maravall asks "so when can Spanish politics return to normal?" after listing its current deficiencies (Maravall, 2007), he is asking when Spain's political culture will return to the guiding spirit of 1978—a spirit that was fully incarnated in the PSOE's 1982 election victory. Spanish politics over the last decade has in his view been an uncomfortable departure from, not an expression of, this spirit. Lassalle even notes approvingly that the 1978 Constitution allowed the Spanish left to develop "in the best tradition of interwar Republicanism" (Lassalle 2016, p. 7), the period Podemos' leaders repeatedly reference when they speak about recovering the best of Spain's democratic traditions. As Lassalle and Maravall see it, the constitution is a model of liberal tolerance that provides ample opportunities for deepening democracy. If Spanish politics has deteriorated then this is the fault of other, more recent, developments—the emergence of Podemos among them.

In 1996 sociologist Juan Linz began his and Alfred Stepan's seminal account of Spain's shift from dictatorship to democracy with the following words: "There is growing consensus that the Spanish transition is in many ways the paradigmatic case for the study of pacted democratic transition and rapid democratic consolidation, much as the Weimar Republic became

Divergent presents 61

paradigmatic for the study of democratic breakdown" (Linz and Stepan 1996, p. 107). Though he had lived in Spain since 1932, Linz was born under the Weimar Constitution in Bonn in 1926 and had completed extensive research on Germany's plunge into totalitarianism in the 1930s. Once he moved to the USA for his postgraduate studies, Linz even studied under erstwhile leftist Schmittian Otto Kirchheimer, who had himself been one of Schmitt's students before he was forced, like so many other Jewish intellectuals, to flee Germany in 1932. Over his lifetime, Linz acquired an unparalleled authority in Spain to pronounce on the quality of the country's democracy, becoming, as Duncan Wheeler puts it, "the founding father of canonical accounts of the transition" (Wheeler 2017, p. 456). In the first decades after 1978 his casting of Weimar Germany and post-transition Spain as polar opposites achieved the status of common sense.

As early as 2012—long before Podemos existed but as its precursor, the *indignados* protests, took to the streets once again—Lassalle compared the anti-legal and anti-parliamentarian fervour in Spain to Schmitt's critique of the Weimar Government (Lassalle, 2012). Spreading across the country was, in his view, "an anti-legal and anti-parliamentary hostility that reproduces almost millimetrically the critiques that Schmitt directed in the 1920s and 1930s towards the constitutional state, the primacy of the law, the Weimar constitution and the politicians that defended it" (2012). Two years later, soon after Podemos won five of 54 Spanish seats in the European Parliament, Lassalle wrote that "the elections ... place Spain and Europe on the edge of the abyss of Weimar" (Lassalle, 2014). If contemporary Spain bore any resemblance to Weimar Germany, then this was not a cause but rather partly a *consequence* of Podemos' populist politics.

How similar contemporary Spain is to Weimar Germany is evidently a deeply contested issue within Spanish politics. Stacking up the similarities and differences alongside each other to see which pile is higher seems condemned to inconclusiveness as a consequence; which pile looks higher will inevitably depend on where you stand. What's more important for our purposes is to get a closer look at the vantage point from which Iglesias and Errejón see Spain's present; how we understand the present is, after all, a function of both how we see the past and how we see the future. Only once we have reconstructed the complete narrative structuring the Podemos leaders' political vision—a narrative that joins together past, present and future—will it be possible to fully understand their concern that the instability and political impotence of Schmitt's time is being reproduced in their own.

In the next two chapters we will try to uncover Iglesias' and Errejón's existing personal-political narrative. This narrative tells a story not just about the origins of contemporary politics in Spain, but also about where

62 Divergent presents

Spanish politics might—in their view—ideally end up. It is a narrative in which Iglesias and Errejón position themselves as two of the story's authors, as active participants in determining its trajectory. It thus fuses together the personal and the political in a dynamic understanding of the present that extends into both the past and the future. In order to understand why Schmitt's ideas have resonated with Iglesias and Errejón, we need to see how these ideas fit into the structure of the Podemos leaders' pre-existing narrative. We might understand resonance as resulting partly from a homology of narrative structures—a similar alignment of characters, themes and plots. Once we have laid bare the structure of Iglesias' and Errejón's personal-political narrative, it will become clear how closely it resembles the structure of Schmitt's story about politics.

References

Anson, Luis María. 2005. "La lucidez de Mayor Oreja". *La Razón*, 11 April. Available at www.lbouza.net/ESPANA/anson39.htm. Last accessed 27 February 2018.

Bendersky, Joseph. 2014. *Carl Schmitt: Theorist for the Reich.* Princeton, NJ: Princeton University Press.

Bullivant, Keith. 1985. "The conservative revolution". In *The Weimar Dilemma: Intellectuals in the Weimar Republic.* Edited by Anthony Phelan. Manchester: Manchester University Press.

Cumin, David. 2005. *Carl Schmitt: Biographie politique et intellectuelle.* Paris: Éditions du cerf.

della Porta, Donatella, Hara Kouki and Joseba Fernández. 2017. "Left's Love and Hate for Europe: Syriza, Podemos and Critical Visions of Europe During the Crisis". In *Euroscepticism, Democracy and the Media.* Edited by Manuela Caiani and Simona Guerra. London: Palgrave Macmillan.

Doncel, Luis. 2016. "Alemania presiona para que España reciba un castigo ejemplarizante". *El País*, 5 July.

Errejón, Íñigo. 2012. *La lucha por la hegemonía durante el primer gobierno del MAS en Bolivia (2006–2009): un análisis discursivo.* Doctoral thesis (unpublished). Faculty of Political Sciences and Sociology, Complutense University of Madrid.

Errejón, Íñigo. 2015c. "Crisis de régimen y hegemonía". *La Circular*, 10 April. Available at http://lacircular.info/crisis-de-regimen-y-hegemonia/. Last accessed 27 February 2018.

Errejón, Íñigo and Chantal Mouffe. 2016. *Podemos: In the Name of the People.* London: Lawrence & Wishart.

Gaab, Jeffrey S. 2006. *Munich: Hofbräuhaus & History – Beer, Culture, & Politics.* Oxford: Peter Lang.

Gay, Peter. 2001. *Weimar: The Outsider as Insider.* London: W. W. Norton & Company.

Divergent presents 63

Hoelzl, Michael and Graham Ward. 2014. "Translators' Introduction". In *Dictatorship: from the origin of the modern concept of sovereignty to proletarian class struggle*, by Carl Schmitt. Cambridge: Polity Press.

Iglesias, Pablo. 2014a. *Disputar la democracia: política para tiempos de crisis.* Madrid: Ediciones Akal.

Iglesias, Pablo. 2015a. *Una nueva Transición: materiales del año del cambio.* Second Edition. Madrid: Ediciones Akal.

Kennedy, Ellen. 2004. *Constitutional Failure: Carl Schmitt in Weimar.* Durham, NC and London: Duke University Press.

Laqueur, Walter. 1974. *Weimar: A Cultural History 1918–1933.* London: Weidenfeld & Nicolson.

Lassalle, Jose María. 2012. "Antipolítica y multitud". *El País*, 1 October.

Lassalle, José María. 2014. "España en Weimar o Bolivia". *El País*, 2 June.

Lassalle, José María. 2016. "Apertura del seminario: Las urgencias de la libertad". *Nueva Revista de Política, Cultura y Arte*, 156. pp. 6–16.

Lassalle, José María. 2017. *Contra el populismo: Cartografía de un totalitarismo posmoderno.* Digital edition (Amazon Kindle). Barcelona: Penguin Random House.

Linz, Juan J. and Alfred Stepan. 1996. *Problems of Democratic Transition and Consolidation: Southern Europe, South America, and Post-Communist Europe.* Baltimore, MD: The Johns Hopkins University Press.

López García, José Antonio. 1996. "La presencia de Carl Schmitt en España". *Revista de Estudios Políticos*, 91. pp. 139–168.

Maravall, José María. 2007. "La crispación". *El País*, 7 May.

Maravall, José María. 2013a. *Las promesas políticas.* Barcelona: Galaxia Gutenberg.

Maravall, José María. 2013b. "La hostilidad respecto de los partidos". *El País*, 24 February.

Maravall, José María. 2016. *Demands on Democracy.* Oxford: Oxford University Press.

Marsili, Lorenzo and Jorge Moruno. 2016. "Podemos: reclaiming Europe is a revolutionary slogan". *OpenDemocracy*, 17 June. Available at www.opendemocra cy.net/can-europe-make-it/lorenzo-marsili-jorge-moruno/podemos-reclaim ing-europe-is-revolutionary-slogan. Last accessed 27 February 2018.

McCormick, John. 2009. *Carl Schmitt's Critique of Liberalism: Against Politics as Technology.* Cambridge: Cambridge University Press.

Mehring, Reinhard. 2014. *Carl Schmitt: A Biography.* Translated by Daniel Steuer. Cambridge: Polity Press.

Muller, Jerry Z. 1991. "Carl Schmitt, Hans Freyer and the Radical Conservative Critique of Liberal Democracy in the Weimar Republic". *History of Political Thought*, 12(4). pp. 695–715.

Reig Tapia, Alberto. 2016. "¿Un nuevo fracaso histórico? La transición a la democracia, el Rey Juan Carlos I y el derecho a decidir". In *Transiciones en el mundo contemporáneo.* Edited by Alberto Reig Tapia and Josep Sánchez Cervelló. Tarragona / Mexico City: Publicacions Universitat Rovira i Virgili / Universidad Nacional Autónoma de México.

64 *Divergent presents*

Rodríguez, Marta and Alfonso L. Congostrina. 2017. "La Generalitat cifra en 844 los atendidos por heridas y ataques de ansiedad". *El País*, 2 October.

Rohkrämer, Thomas. 2007. *A Single Communal Faith: The German Right from Conservatism to National Socialism*. New York: Berghahn.

Schmitt, Carl. 1926. "Diktatur". In *Staatslexikon im Auftrage der Görresgesellschaft, Vol.1*. Freiburg: Herder. pp. 1448–1453.

Schmitt, Carl. 1988. *The Crisis of Parliamentary Democracy*. Boston, MA: MIT Press.

Schmitt, Carl. 2006. *Political Theology: Four Chapters on the Concept of Sovereignty*. Chicago, IL: University of Chicago Press.

Schmitt, Carl. 2007a. *The Concept of the Political*. Expanded Edition. Translated by George Schwab. London: University of Chicago Press.

Schmitt, Carl. 2013. *Dictatorship*. Cambridge: Polity Press.

Storer, Colin. 2013. *A Short History of the Weimar Republic*. London: I. B. Tauris.

Taubes, Jacob. 2013. *To Carl Schmitt: Letters and Reflections*. New York: Columbia University Press.

Torreblanca, José Ignacio. 2015. *Asaltar los cielos: Podemos o la política después de la crisis*. Second Edition. Barcelona: Penguin Random House.

Unidos Podemos. 2016. *Programa*. Available at https://lasonrisadeunpais.es/programa/.

Wheeler, Duncan. 2017. "The Generation Game: Javier Cercas, Podemos and the (Im)Possibility of Progressive Politics in Spain". *MLN* 132:2. pp. 441–460.

Wolin, Richard. 1992. "Carl Schmitt, the conservative revolutionary habitus and the aesthetics of horror". *Political Theory* 20:3. pp. 438–444.

4 Imagining the political past

Teasing out the similarities between Weimar Germany and contemporary Spain may help explain why the Podemos intellectuals appropriated certain aspects of Schmitt's thought. Doing so goes some way to explaining why Schmitt's writings might have resonated with them as readers, and why left-wing variants of some of his political solutions might have seemed appealing. It is not too difficult to see how Schmitt's opposition of the sovereign people to the liberal elites, his emphasis on public and collective politics against a narrowly economised life, and his relegation of the constitution to a position below the people's will all fit quite widespread political narratives in contemporary Spain, as they did in Weimar Germany. But there are other aspects of Schmitt's thought taken up by Podemos that seem anathema to a mainstream progressive political force operating under conditions otherwise so unlike those Schmitt lived through. Among these are his assertion that violence is beneath all politics and the bellicose metaphors that follow; his conviction that enemies must be excluded; and his emphasis on specifically pro-national patriotic sentiment. Spain is not, as Weimar Germany was, in the grips of an armed power struggle between extremists and moderates. It has not recently been a belligerent in a global war. But there is a historical narrative at play in Spanish politics that, once better understood, makes Podemos' appropriation of Schmitt's ideas both less puzzling and all the more interesting.

Something of this narrative is woven through the biography of Juan Donoso Cortés, who Schmitt refers to as "one of the foremost representatives of decisionist thinking" (Schmitt 2005, pp. 51–2). Via Cortés, this historical narrative about Spanish politics may even have influenced Schmitt's view of Weimar Germany—which raises the possibility that Schmitt's work is intrinsically keyed into Spanish political narrative structures. Cortés was born in 1809, the year after the French invaded the Iberian peninsula and deposed Ferdinand VII, who had been King for only forty-eight days following his father's abdication. Napoleon—by now an

66 *Imagining the political past*

enemy of the Pope—had installed his brother, Joseph Bonaparte, on the Spanish throne. Out of the resulting opposition to the Bonapartes' six-year rule emerged Spain's first attempt at sovereign government by an assembly of representatives: the Cádiz Cortes. In 1810 the Cortes—composed of nobles and clergymen but also liberal middle-class intellectuals such as Gaspar Melchor de Jovellanos—met for the first time. From the outset its members proposed that the Cortes, rather than the King, should be considered sovereign, since the Cortes represented the people. It was the people, "the nation", not the monarch, who had sovereignty over all the kingdoms within the Monarchy of Spain (Cádiz Cortes, 1812). With a liberal majority, the Cortes was able to enact the Spanish Constitution of 1812, which sought to limit the executive powers of the monarchy, subjecting them to parliamentary scrutiny. Article 172 of the 1812 constitution details "restrictions upon the regal authority". It specifies that under no circumstances can the King prevent, suspend or dissolve the meeting of the Cortes, nor can he dispossess any corporation or person of property, nor "punish, in any manner whatsoever, or deprive any individual of his liberty"—though it does allow that in the event of treason or an "attempt against the security of the State" the King may "give directions for personal arrests" (Cádiz Cortes, 1812).

Though Spain's army failed to push back Napoleon's forces in the Cortes' early years, by 1812 the French had been weakened by their defeat in Russia and were eventually forced out of the peninsula in 1814 with help from the British and Portuguese. When Ferdinand VII returned to the throne he and his conservative allies in the Cortes immediately did away with the constitution, re-establishing an absolute monarchy with sovereignty over Spain and her colonies. But the *criollos* in South America had already taken advantage of their colonial power's weakness after 1808, and had begun a series of revolts that would successfully shake off European rule in the decade that followed. Unable to pay the soldiers that he sent to suppress the South American uprisings, Ferdinand was forced to accept the 1812 constitution in 1820 when, unpaid by its bankrupt King, the Spanish military revolted. A liberal government managed to rule for three years before France invaded again—this time in support of Ferdinand—and bombarded Cádiz until parliament conceded defeat and dissolved the Cortes. Ferdinand took back his absolute power, and revoked the constitution. For the next fifty years—until the start of the First Spanish Republic in 1873—Spain experienced a succession of armed struggles between conservatives and reformists, with each side represented by their own claimants to the throne.

Though the struggles between Ferdinand and the liberals occurred while Donoso was a child, it was as a child that Donoso began his university

Imagining the political past 67

education. By the age of 12, in 1821, he was studying law at the University of Salamanca. At first quite taken with the liberal cause, over time Donoso became increasingly disillusioned with the liberals' approach as he witnessed their inability to confront the messy reality of Spain's divisions. By the time he visited Berlin in 1848, soon after the revolutions of that year swept through Europe, Donoso's outlook had become decidedly conservative. It is this shift that Schmitt captured in his 1928 article *Donoso Cortés in Berlin*, written just before he moved to the city himself. Schmitt pointed out that Donoso might have started off as a liberal political theorist of the state, but he had gradually moved to the right and become a staunch defender of a conservative dictatorship. Though ostensibly a historical work about Donoso, Schmitt liked to draw parallels between himself and the Spaniard; in *Donoso Cortés in Berlin*, there is an obvious link between his depiction of the main protagonist and Schmitt's own programme of constitutional policy (Mehring 2014, p. 200).

It was partly Donoso's realism that appealed to Schmitt (cf. Schmitt 2007a, p. 61). "What Donoso Cortés had to say about the natural depravity and vileness of man", Schmitt wrote in *Political Theology*, "was indeed more horrible than anything that had ever been alleged by an absolutist philosophy of the state in justifying authoritarian rule" (p. 58). His view of history was correspondingly bleak, "full of dread and horror" (p. 59). Yet all the liberals did in the face of this bloody reality was talk. Schmitt approvingly quotes Donoso's definition of the bourgeoisie as "a 'discussing class', *una clase discutidora*"—a definition that "contains the class characteristic of wanting to evade the decision" (p. 59). Liberalism, with its assumption that freedom of speech and of the press will solve all problems, that "truth will emerge automatically through voting", was nothing but "a cautious half measure" that hopelessly tried to sidestep "the decisive bloody battle" by transforming it into an everlasting discussion in which the decision is "suspended forever" (p. 63). It was because Donoso recognised this that he arrived at the doctrine Schmitt would later call his own: decisionism.

Iglesias and Errejón's background

To understand why Schmitt has had particular appeal for Iglesias and Errejón, it is necessary to understand not just how Schmitt's ideas resonate with Spain's history, but how they resonate with Iglesias and Errejón's particular *interpretation* of Spain's history and present. Some idea of this interpretation can be gleaned from what they have said or written in the past, but much can also be inferred by looking at the diet of historical memory they are likely to have consumed at various times in their lives.

68   *Imagining the political past*

Doing this is not entirely straightforward, however. The interpretation of Spain's past has been heavily politicised throughout the Podemos leaders' lifetime. Building up an accurate picture of Iglesias' and Errejón's own historical memory requires knowledge not just of their own biographies but also of the biography of historical memory in Spain since the 1970s.

Iglesias and Errejón were born five years apart, both in Madrid. They grew up in families for whom the Civil War was very much still alive. Errejón's family was persecuted under Francoism and his father—an activist with the Partido del Trabajo de España (Spanish Workers' Party) and later the Izquierda Anticapitalista (Anticapitalist Left), now part of Podemos—was a political prisoner of the regime (Errejón and Mouffe 2016, p. 118). Iglesias' father—a retired history teacher—was also "familiar with Caraban-chel [the jail used by Franco for political prisoners] because he distributed propaganda" (Iglesias 2015a, p. 75). "I grew up in a family with memory", Iglesias wrote in *El País* in June 2015, "in which my grandmother never stopped telling me about the shooting of her brother, a socialist, in 1939. I am the grandson of someone condemned to death, also a socialist, whose sentence was finally commuted to 30 years of which he served five. My parents were militant communists when in Spain this was a crime" (p. 75). Iglesias' mother, a lawyer for a major trade union, told *El País* that the working class struggle had been part of the family "since the nineteenth century". The slogan of the Podemos intellectuals' political talk-show, *La Tuerka*, could equally be a family motto: "without fear and with memory".

It was at the Complutense University of Madrid (UCM) that Iglesias and Errejón met. Having already completed an undergraduate degree in law, in 2002 Iglesias started a new degree in Political Sciences, graduating in 2004. Two years later, Errejón graduated from the same course. Both went on to do doctoral work under the same supervisor, Heriberto Cairo Carou (Rivero 2015, p. 45), a specialist in Latin American politics and international relations. Political scientist José Ignacio Torreblanca describes the Complutense as an institution in which students are always mobilising around some cause or other, frequently protesting to protect what they see as minority or marginalised interests against the establishment. Despite their best attempts, the authorities have been unable to enforce rules that would prohibit smoking or prevent drinking outside the bar. They have been "obliged to tolerate" even "irregular or straightforwardly illegal practices" such as the sale of food, tobacco and drinks by the students or the setting up of stalls advertising support for terrorist groups such as the Basque separatist group Euskadi Ta Askatasuna (ETA) (Torreblanca 2015, pp. 84–5).

While pursuing their doctorates at the Complutense, Iglesias and Errejón both became involved in a think tank called the Fundación Centro de Estudios Políticos y Sociales (CEPS). In its own words, CEPS' work aims

Imagining the political past 69

to help build "a bridge between the emancipatory experiences of Latin America and the attempts at constructing counterhegemonic left-wing politics in Europe" (Torreblanca 2015, p. 95). As part of his work for CEPS, Iglesias advised the Venezuelan government. Errejón, meanwhile, worked for a Venezuelan research organisation directed by Jesse Chacón, a former general who had participated in Chávez' attempted coup of 1992. Juan Carlos Monedero, a Complutense professor of political science who would later help Iglesias and Errejón found Podemos, was responsible for an arm of CEPS that sought to be the preeminent international hub of knowledge about Venezuela's "revolutionary transformations" (Torreblanca 2015, p. 93). Allegations have even been made that in 2008 Venezuela funnelled money through CEPS specifically to encourage the establishment of a political party—the outcome of which was allegedly Podemos (Burgen 2016). In April 2016 the Spanish national daily ABC published what it believed was "definitive proof" that "Podemos was born as an extension of Chavismo in Spain" (Chicote 2016). Though none of these accusations has stuck, they only got off the ground because of the close proximity of Podemos' leaders to Latin American politics, not just as academics but as consultant-activists.

The Complutense offered plenty of other opportunities for political engagement, of which Iglesias—who had already been an activist with the Juventudes Comunistas (Communist Youth) since the age of 14—took full advantage. In 2006, along with other figures who would play a prominent role in Podemos' birth including Errejón, he helped founded the collective Asociación Contrapoder (Counter-power Association) in the Faculty of Political Sciences and Sociology at the Complutense. Contrapoder was a collective of left-wing, anti-capitalist and internationalist activists. Its inaugural act was to announce through a megaphone in the faculty cafeteria that its members were planning to paint a huge mural of Tommie Smith and John Carlos, the two black athletes who raised their fists at the 1968 Olympics, on an internal wall. Its purpose was to create a space of "disobedience" at the Complutense (Torreblanca 2015, pp. 86–7). In 2009 the collective teamed up with CEPS to invite the president of "the Plurinational State of Bolivia", Evo Morales, to speak at the UCM; when Morales arrived he was presented with a large mural of Tupac Katari, leader of one of the most significant indigenous rebellions against the Spanish Empire (Errejón and Iglesias 2009). A year later Contrapoder organised protests against the appearance of social-democrat-turned-free-market politician Rosa Díez at a UCM conference (Campelo 2010).

Torreblanca leads us through what he calls the semantic flirtation with violence present in Contrapoder's manifesto. "Clashes and losses are natural consequences of engaging with the enemy", it reads. "The powerful

70 *Imagining the political past*

yield nothing, they are not going to abandon the stage of history without a fight, and for this reason there are no alternatives to battle". The manifesto adds that "on many occasions violence has been a necessary weapon of the hope of liberation: we consider it a tool". "We desire a world without violence", the authors conclude, "but any position that prefers to renounce emancipatory violence over attacking ... the structural violence of hunger, of the fragile boats of migrants, of wars, of poverty, of prisons and the alienation of man (and of woman!) from his natural and social environment, is unethical" (Contrapoder 2006; Torreblanca 2015, p. 88).

Beyond the experience of activism, it was at the Complutense that another critical part of the Podemos leaders' training for life in contemporary politics began. In 2007, Iglesias helped organise and chaired a series of debates in the faculty called *99 seconds*, out of which came the opportunity to host the TV chat show *La Tuerka* (Rivero 2015 p. 94). Participating in the first edition of *99 seconds*, entitled "The left to the left of the PSOE [Spanish Socialist Workers' Party]", were members of various significant political parties, including Izquierda Anticapitalista, Iniciativa Internationalista, Izquierda Unida and the Bloque Nacionalista Galego. Paco Pérez, presenter and director of Madrid community TV station Tele K, was in the audience, and was sufficiently impressed to offer Iglesias a slot on his channel. With the help of both Errejón and Monedero, Iglesias launched his weekly show *La Tuerka* on Tele K in November 2010. As the programme's quality and accessibility increased it jumped to YouTube, where it reached a much larger audience. *La Tuerka* was born, as Iglesias put it, "from frustration and boredom with academic acts, which are unable to create 'frames [of reference]'" (Torreblanca 2015, p. 103). Within academia, you can debate all you like but your thoughts may lead nowhere; "television", by contrast "is to contemporary politics what gunpowder was to war" (Torreblanca 2015, p. 107).

These formative experiences may go some way to explaining Errejón's and Iglesias' taste for the bellicose. But it is only on building up a detailed picture of how these experiences have combined with interpretations of Spain's political past and present that the Podemos leaders' affinity with Schmitt can be properly understood. On the face of it, Spain's history does not make it too difficult to gather material for a Schmittian interpretation of politics. In Spain, war remains "the past that has not passed away" (Graham 2012, p. 11); even though the Civil War took place nearly eighty years ago, it is still an indelible part of Spain's self-understanding. And the Francoist regime that followed "constitutes", in Helen Graham's words, "the most significant and enduring 'Western' example of how European polities, societies and 'nations' of the mid-twentieth century came to be reconstructed through violence" (2012, p. 22). In this sense Spain is

Imagining the political past 71

indeed an "abnormal or exceptional country with respect to the rest of Europe", despite Podemos analyst Torreblanca's claim to the contrary (Torreblanca 2015, p. 44). We cannot properly understand "the Podemos phenomenon" as "the product of a generalised situation in our continent", as he suggests, but must understand it as partly the product of a geographically-specific set of historical memories refracted through its leaders' experiences (p. 45).

The history of memory in Spain

Iglesias' and Errejón's formative political experiences took place at a time when Spain was only just beginning to remember the violence of its past after years of intentional forgetting. After Franco's death in 1975, political elites agreed formally to an amnesty law that granted immunity for all political crimes committed prior to 1977 (see Preston 2006, pp. 11–12; Casanova and Andrés 2014, pp. 310ff.; Jimeno 2017). Informally, they also entered into what has become known as the Pact of Forgetting, agreeing not even to speak about the Civil War of 1936–39 and the reprisals that followed its end—unless it was to lament their unfortunate, fratricidal character (see also Núñez Seixas 2017, pp. 152ff.; Casanova and Andrés 2014, pp. 310–311). The purpose of this transitional amnesia was not just to erase memories of the bloodletting of the past forty years; it was also to redirect Spaniards' minds permanently towards the future and away from what might have seemed like their country's inherent inability to stabilise politically (see also Phillips and Rahn Phillips 2012, p. 296). Though a political pact can evidently not forcibly erase a population's memories, it can place such a taboo on the appearance of certain claims in public discourse that some arguments—and thus some political strategies—become almost impossible (see Aguilar and Payne 2016, p. 8). Along with the Pact came a spirit of a "new beginning", an ethos of "national reconciliation", a plea for "political moderation" and a call for the primacy of reason over violence (Desfor Eldes 2010, pp. 41–62).

The 1936 *franquista* coup against the Second Republic that precipitated the Civil War was only the latest violent turn of political events since the 1860s. The first Spanish Republic, established in 1873 after five bloody years, was extinguished by a military coup in 1874 (Phillips and Rahn Phillips 2012, pp. 223ff.). After the forty-year mock-democracy that followed, in which liberal and conservative parties simply took turns in governing, another military coup put in place the repressive dictatorship of Primo de Rivera in 1923. 1931's Second Republic lasted a little longer than the First, but not by much (pp. 239–250). Following Franco's death it might have seemed as if Spain could leave this violence behind, but in

72 *Imagining the political past*

February 1981—with the new constitution of 1978 only three years old— an attempted military coup convinced many Spaniards that active suppression of an apparently ingrained characteristic was the only path towards progress. This could only be achieved by the rejection of introspection grounded in Spain's violent history and the embrace of an extroversion backed by a vision of the future that lay outside Spain itself, in the European project. Once again the political elite was invoking José Ortega y Gasset's dictum that "Spain is the problem, Europe is the solution".

In the 1980s, European integration presented opportunities for Spaniards to buy into the kind of modern Western lifestyle they had previously been denied, diverting attention away from the politics of the past (Labanyi 2007, p. 94). "Consumerism", Helen Graham claims, "was being posited as an alternative to democratic memory itself" (Graham 2012, p. 150). But Europeanisation did not just offer a way for Spaniards to distract themselves from the violence of their history; it also *required* Spaniards to perform as though this history were not part of their present. From the outset, the European project had peace within and between nations at its core. By suppressing memories of its past and emphasising the stability of its Transition, Spain could present itself as the model European nation—one that had decisively cast off any vestiges of backwardness. In 1986, the year that Spain joined the European Economic Community (EEC, now European Union) and the fiftieth anniversary of Franco's coup, the PSOE government issued a statement claiming that "the Civil War is history and no longer a part of the reality of the country" (Encarnación 2014, pp. 79–83).

And yet the need to make such a statement clearly belies the truth of its claim. A pact to forget is not the same as individual forgetting (see Aguilar 2007, p. 2); it is merely the stage for a performance of forgetting that requires memory for its foundation. It was only because memory of the Civil War was so deeply embedded that this performance of forgetting could succeed, gaining the complicity of the vast majority of the Spanish population. Under Franco's regime, the psychological wounds of the war had been deepened deliberately even while the possibility of the Republican side being moved into action by their memory was eliminated. "Nunca más", (never again), Franco proclaimed as he exaggerated the number of those killed in the war: "un millón de muertos" (a million dead) (Encarnación 2014, p. 43). By constantly refreshing Spaniards' memory of violence, the Franco regime could present itself as the only stable hand able to keep the nation from relapsing into its natural state of anarchic civil war (p. 47). After Franco's death this memory persevered with such force that Adolfo Suárez, a key minister in the *franquista* regime's dotage, could become Spain's first democratically-elected prime minister and remain in position for the next six years without his legitimacy being undermined by his

Imagining the political past 73

proximity to the dictatorship. That violence continued to erupt across the country during this period only strengthened Spaniards' resolve to bind the wounds of the past in amnesia (Aguilar and Payne 2016, p. 8).

The attempted coup in 1981 on the last day of Suárez's premiership only served to revive the fears of civil war that Franco kept alive through memory, strengthening the political elites and their message that to go on into the future required the complete suppression of the past. Though the coup attempt failed, its most dramatic denouement—an armed incursion into the Spanish parliament led by Lieutenant-Colonel Antonio Tejero— was broadcast live on television (Phillips and Rahn Phillips 2012, pp. 283– 284). Only three years earlier a planned military coup had been discovered just two weeks before it took place; this latest attempt could not, then, be dismissed as the plot of a single isolated group (Casanova and Andrés 2014, pp. 319ff.). Following what became known as *El Tejerazo*, a survey showed that 61.5% of the Spanish population feared the outbreak of another civil war in its wake (Centro de Investigaciones Sociológicas 2008, p. 24). Television also brought news of the unrest in neighbouring Portugal, where the transition from dictatorship to democracy after Salazar's death in 1974 produced scenes reminiscent to Spaniards of the events that had helped trigger Franco's 1936 coup: mass mobilisations, land seizures and business expropriations (Encarnación 2014, p. 63). As sociologist Salvador Cardús i Ros suggests, those who orchestrated the Transition required a "clearly defined adversary" against which they could set their new "democratic memory"—one that would draw attention away from former Francoists themselves, since they remained part of the political elite. Tejero provided the perfect candidate, as well as the perfect dramatic backdrop for Francoists to set themselves publicly against this new enemy (Cardús i Ros 2000, p. 26). When the armed Tejero burst into the parliament chamber with a *Guardia Civil* unit, 68-year-old Minister of Defence General Gutiérrez Mellado, a prominent military figure who had fought on Franco's side during the civil war, rose to his feet to remonstrate with the intruders (Phillips and Rahn Phillips 2012, p. 283). Their failed attempt to wrestle him to the ground became a potent symbol of the new democracy's resilience in the face of a threat that united Francoists and their opponents.

It was primarily fear, then, that lay behind the Pact of Forgetting's success—a fear of war's recurrence that depended on "the memory of murder" (Graham 2012, p. 71, p. 127; also Preston 2006, p. 9). But there were other factors that made a Pact of Forgetting particularly attractive both to ordinary people and to the political élites, among which was a fear of justice itself. Although those on the left might, given that the Nationalists were overwhelmingly more violent than the Republicans, have been expected to want to see some kind of restorative justice following Franco's

74 *Imagining the political past*

death, even as late as 2008 a national poll showed that the majority of respondents believed the Nationalists and Republicans killed the same number of people during the Civil War (35.9%), and that the left and right were equally to blame for its occurrence (39.9%) (Centro de Investigaciones Sociológicas 2008, pp. 13–14). These figures reflect how little accurate information circulated about the Civil War and its aftermath under the Franco regime, including in school history textbooks of the period. Propaganda aimed at both adults and children portrayed the war as a religious crusade against the horrors of Communism long into the 1960s, and ceremonial burials of fallen Nationalists kept atrocities committed in the Republican zones in the public eye (Preston 2006, p. 4, p. 11). If anyone was to be brought to justice for what had happened during the war, it might have been thought equally likely to be those on the left as those on the right; neither side, then, had much appetite in the 1970s and 1980s for exhuming the war's atrocities in justice's name. The same went for those crimes committed in the years after the war under the *franquista* regime. Though only a small minority directly perpetrated the regime's violent politically-motivated reprisals, hundreds of thousands of Spaniards were indirectly complicit in these crimes because they had denounced people they knew to the authorities (Graham 2012, p. 22). Given that a significant proportion of the Spanish population believed they had something to fear from a full airing of the past forty years' misdeeds, it was not difficult for them to endorse a performance of forgetting (see Aguilar and Payne 2016, p. 6).

For similar reasons, forgetting made obvious sense for those elites who had participated directly in Franco's regime. There would be no prosecution for the assassinations, disappearances and imprisonment of Republicans and their sympathisers. Democratisation combined with collective forgetting would allow them to remain in the highest echelons of politics without worrying about being branded unfit to hold political power. Forgetting also made sense for elites on the left. Many left-wing leaders had radical backgrounds, and although the Nationalist side was responsible for the overwhelming majority of killings during the Civil War and its aftermath, this was not clear at the time, and the left also had blood on its hands. The Pact of Forgetting enabled those who might under ordinary circumstances have been excluded from politics by their violent pasts to gain a seat at the negotiating table. But political amnesia was also convenient for those with too *little* blood on their hands: the PSOE, who had provided little resistance to the Franco regime from exile abroad, were happy to have their relative inaction forgotten (Encarnación 2014, p. 28, pp. 60–61).

Perhaps even more important for the left's support of active forgetting was its enthusiasm for the European political project (see also Desfor Eldes 2010, pp. 56–58). Suppressed under Franco, leaders of the left's biggest

Imagining the political past 75

political party, the PSOE, had passed the years of the dictatorship exiled in Paris. They had begun to see Europe as the solution to Spain's problems—but to join the European club, Spain had to demonstrate its economic stability, and economic stability required political stability. Political stability was not, however, what history would indicate should be associated with the left—quite the opposite. The two Republics of 1873–74 and 1931–36 had been the least politically stable peacetime periods in the last hundred years. It was convenient, then, for the left to have this part of Spanish history politically forgotten along with the Civil War itself and the repression that followed.

For two decades the Pact of Forgetting lasted almost unchallenged. But in 1998 Spain's political amnesia was disturbed by an event that took place beyond the country's borders: the arrest of Chile's former dictator, Augusto Pinochet. Although Pinochet was arrested in London, the warrant for his arrest was issued by a Spanish judge whose name would later become emblematic of Spain's "memory wars", Baltasar Garzón. Garzón and his colleague Manuel García-Castellón had acted after considering a case brought before them under the principle of *acción popular*, which allows any Spanish citizen to suggest that the courts open a case they believe to be in the public interest (Encarnación 2014, p. 134). The charge against Pinochet was suspected genocide and terrorism.

Soon after Pinochet's arrest, the Chilean government issued a statement claiming that his detention was a violation of diplomatic immunity. Chilean president Eduardo Frei accused Spain of hypocrisy: how could it have the arrogance to reopen another sovereign country's wounds in the name of justice when it had no intention of reopening its own (El País 1998)? Spain's own prime minister and leader of the conservative PP (Partido Popular—People's Party, a grouping whose predecessor was founded by ex-*franquistas*, as Pablo Iglesias has not hesitated to remind its current members (Iglesias 2016)) José María Aznar declined to side with the Spanish courts on the issue—he described the arrest as an example of judicial overreach—and even former socialist leader Felipe González, Prime Minister from 1982–96, opposed Pinochet's extradition to Spain (Encarnación 2014, pp. 140–44).

Meanwhile, mass protests were taking place across Spain demanding that Pinochet be extradited to and tried there rather than in Chile, where in his post as a life-long senator—a position he himself had created—Chilean law gave him immunity from prosecution. Perhaps influenced by reports of the results of truth commissions in South America that were headline news at the time, many Spaniards seemed to have developed an appetite for bringing past political crimes back into public discourse. Editorials and op-eds in Spanish newspapers began to observe a process of psychological transference at work; Pinochet's arrest, they suggested, represented what many

76 *Imagining the political past*

Spaniards wished could have happened with Franco, who had "disappeared" and killed many more than Pinochet ever had (Graham 2012, p. 11). The PSOE's new leadership was less reluctant than the old guard to give expression to this thought. "If only we could have done the same with Franco", PSOE spokesman Alfredo Pérez Rubalcaba remarked (Malamud 2003, p. 157).

Pinochet's arrest cleaved open a rift not just between left and right, but between an older political elite on the left—those who had participated in the Transition—and a younger group of left-wing politicians like Rubalcaba whose political careers had begun in the post-Transition era. It also precipitated a public discourse of remembering beyond the political class. By 1999 the Aznar government had begun to receive requests for support in exhuming and reburying the remains of those killed by Franco's regime. In 2000 Emilio Silva, a young journalist perplexed as to why Spaniards were so interested in prosecuting Pinochet but not in investigating similar acts committed by Franco, established the Asociación para la Recuperación de la Memoria Histórica (Association for the Recovery of Historical Memory, ARMH) (Renshaw 2016, pp. 17–25). Silva's ARMH would support families wishing to exhume the bodies of their relatives assassinated by the Nationalists during the Civil War. To this end the organisation not only raised money to support the exhumations; it also collected many oral histories from those alive during the war, which were picked up and published by the press. In 2006, virtual exhumations started to take place in the pages of Spanish newspapers as notices honouring those who had died during the war and its aftermath began to appear: Republicans were memorialised in liberal papers such as *El País*; Nationalists in conservative papers such as *El Mundo* (Encarnación 2014, pp. 146–54). These "obituary wars", as they became known, signalled an irreparable tear in the fabric of ordinary Spaniards' public amnesia. A year later it became clear that the public amnesia of the political elites had undergone comparable damage.

In 2004 the PSOE had come back to power after eight years of PP rule. Its leader was José Luis Rodríguez Zapatero, whose entire political career had taken place after the Transition. Zapatero's government—which took as its intellectual manifesto philosopher Philip Pettit's "Civic Republicanism" (Martí and Pettit 2010)—set about dismantling the Pact of Forgetting. In its first year, the PSOE government established a Memorial Commission tasked with assessing "the situation of the victims of the Civil War and of *franquismo*" and chaired by the deputy Prime Minister. The Commission would report on these victims' rights, on how access to archives could be improved so as to "bring about the closure sought", and on how a bill might be constructed that would offer "adequate recognition and moral satisfaction" to the victims (Gobierno de España 2004).

Imagining the political past 77

In 2007 the PSOE under Zapatero passed the Law of Historical Memory which, for the first time, lifted the amnesty and enabled grievances generated during both the Civil War and the Franco regime to be addressed. Now that those who had fought in the War were passing away along with their "biological memory" (Graham 2012, p. 72), the conflict itself was at last being exhumed. The law was seen by some as permitting the continuation of the Civil War, eighty years on, by symbolic means (cf. Anson 2005); it required public roads with *franquista* names to be renamed and the elimination of Falangist symbols from monuments— though in Helen Graham's words it failed to "offer any means of allowing citizens to address what was actually done to whom, by whom and why", and to a large extent protected perpetrators' right to "privacy" (Graham 2012, p. 147). Under Mariano Rajoy the conservative PP opposed the law, which led to his party being seen by some as Franco's political heir (p. 20).

Memories of the left

Under the climate of public amnesia that followed the 1978 Transition, memories of the Civil War and the Franco regime were largely confined to word-of-mouth stories passed down through families; this is why the ARMH's oral history project in the early 2000s was so significant. Previously such memories had no place in the public domain. It was only in the 1990s that mainstream discourse stopped framing the Civil War as an accident caused by raging passions, and the work of historians who blamed Franco's 1936 uprising became more widely known; and it was also only in the 1990s that research demonstrated conclusively that the number of those killed by the Nationalists was far higher than the number of those killed by the Republicans (Boyd 2008, pp. 136–7). Until the PSOE reformed the curriculum in 1992, even history textbooks glossed over the repression exercised by the Franco regime and presented the Civil War as something for which all sides were culpable (Aguilar 2009, p. 467; Boyd 2008, p. 139). Treglown has done the calculations: "Everyone between roughly forty and their mid-seventies today who was born in Spain was born under Franco, most of them went to school during his regime and almost every man over sixty served in his armed forces" (Treglown 2014, p. 6). Knowledge about this period of Spain's history among adults who grew up under Francoism is usually restricted to whatever was passed on to them by their families (cf. Labanyi 2000, p. 67).

It is not difficult to see how young left-wing political scientists training at the Complutense in Madrid in the early 2000s—when the Pact of Forgetting was crumbling around them—could react against the pact and all that it stood for.[1] They were part of the first cohort of students to have had

78 *Imagining the political past*

almost their entire school education after the 1992 watershed, and also to have been taught at university by teachers whose education took place under democracy (Treglown 2014, p. 131). Whereas twenty years earlier it might have made good political sense to ignore Spain's history and look towards a bright European future, by this point the beliefs and concerns that had grounded this sense no longer applied. Firstly, those in their twenties in the early 2000s had nothing to fear from reprisals, as perhaps their parents' or grandparents' generation had. Secondly, for a long time the military had not shown any evidence of being the volatile force it had been in the late 1970s and early 1980s. Thirdly, and perhaps most importantly, those on the left were no longer faced with a public political discourse that construed each side's struggle in the Civil War as equally illegitimate; the image of the Second Republic had been rehabilitated by historians and blame for the violence that ended it placed squarely on Franco's military coup. As the ARMH's work continued through the 2000s, more and more stories about the atrocities committed by Franco's regime came into public view. Younger survey respondents began consistently to show more negative attitudes towards Franco's regime than their older co-nationals (Treglown 2014, p. 10n). It was becoming possible to argue that the Republican side's military campaign was not only justified, but commendable.

Popular culture may still promote what Iglesias refers to as "reconciliatory discourses of silence" that seek to disperse blame for the Civil War. But students graduating from Iglesias and Errejón's alma mater have proved adept at countering them. It is no coincidence that Emilio Silva, founder of the ARMH, studied in the department of Politics and Sociology at the Complutense. Santos Juliá, one of most prominent historians to have made it their task to correct Spain's historical memory, completed his PhD there. For some time the Complutense has been one of the most abundant sources of what Iglesias refers to as "the antifascist democratic memory that many historians and activists have tried to recuperate" (Iglesias 2015a, p. 33). Even if filmmakers and their ilk have failed to represent "some of the most important historical experiences for understanding Spain's political present" accurately, this has clearly been no obstacle to students at the Complutense who, through historiography and literature, have accessed a version of events from which the Republican left emerges as the clear moral victors (p. 40).

By itself, this version of events might not amount to much. But when set into a longer sweep of Spanish history, its implications gain significance. Although the deal struck during the Transition was motivated by political pragmatism, its legitimacy still depended—at least publicly—on an argument about fairness: since both sides had been equally to blame for the

Imagining the political past 79

war, it was only fair that political crimes on both sides should be forgotten. But once this argument had broken down, the Transition could be interpreted as a settlement achieved not by reasoned deliberation—the liberal-democratic ideal—but by deliberate manipulation, and the 1977 amnesty law Schmitt advocated as illegal (cf. Graham 2012, p. 71). It became more difficult to see Spain's most recent regime as the exception that could be used to rebut the claim that Spanish politics, condemned to descend into an unresolvable dialectic between two opposing factions, was beyond rescue by liberal democracy. If the arguments that underpinned the Transition had been built on a foundation of Francoist propaganda and concealment—itself dependent on the dictatorship's illegitimate power—then the Transition could be set alongside the military coups of 1874, 1923 and 1936 as examples that demonstrated that in Spain the use of force was inextricably bound up with politics.

As late as the year 2000, Cardús i Ros could begin a sociological analysis of the Transition with an explanation of why there had not been any such analysis until now. This was partly because anyone who made the conditions of the Transition explicit "would have weakened [its] legitimacy and even, perhaps, the possibility of its success"—and might have been accused of obstructing democracy's consolidation (Cardús i Ros 2000, p. 18). But by the time Cardús i Ros wrote these words, the circumstances had clearly changed. Democracy no longer seemed under threat; its consolidation had already been successful. Now those on the left could openly criticise the politicians that supposedly represented them for their complicity in a Transition that enabled not just many Franco-era politicians to remain in place, but also members of the civil service, the police force, teachers, university professors and judges who had, "at different times and to different degrees, been accomplices to Franco's regime" (p. 21).

Viewed critically in the light of new historical knowledge, the left that emerged from the Transition did not appear to be the full-blooded left that some wished it were—the left that had existed for short snatches of Spanish history under the First and Second Republics. Next to these bold exemplars it could now seem like only a malnourished imitation. In a political climate where the Republican Government of 1931–36 was understood to bear half of the responsibility for the Civil War, the PSOE had resisted doing anything that might even suggest a return to those years. During the Transition left-wing elites agreed to negotiate behind closed doors in undisclosed locations, deliberately engineering a "tactical demobilisation" of civil society after Suárez convinced them that democracy could be achieved by reforming the regime's institutions rather than breaking with them completely, as the left originally wanted to do (Gunther 2011, p. 30; Ramon Resina 2000, p. 94; Graham 2012, p. 129). These clandestine

80 *Imagining the political past*

discussions resulted in compromises that with hindsight seemed wholly unjust to many on the left: the decision to treat the regime's political prisoners and those who had violently repressed them as equivalent, for example, and the refusal to extend the benefits of the amnesty law to members of the former Republican Army (Aguilar and Payne 2016, pp. 6–7).

When it came to power in 1982, the PSOE looked to Europe for the country's salvation, drifting away from "El Cambio", the redistributive agenda it had promised prior to the election, and driving through a series of neoliberal reforms designed to modernise the economy in preparation for Spain's entry into the EEC. These reforms cost many of the PSOE's traditional working-class supporters their jobs (Encarnación 2014, pp. 86–87). Whilst in government the PSOE also orchestrated the extra-judicial assassination of members of ETA and their sympathisers. The granting of limited autonomy to the Catalans and Basques under the Second Republic had been one of the principal motives for Franco's 1936 military uprising (Ramon Resina 2000, p. 105); by eliminating ETA, the PSOE sought to appease Spain's nationalist tendency. Once the PSOE's post-Transition impurity had been revealed it became easier to see this as a left that had compromised dramatically on its most fundamental principles—as only a distant relation of the democratic left of 1873 and 1931.

By perpetuating the war against ETA, the PSOE were, after all, extending a Francoist policy of repression that exploited the Schmittian concept of exceptionality. As Spain centralised during the sixteenth and seventeenth centuries, the Basque provinces retained their *fueros*—rights to a degree of autonomy—and held on to them even when Catalonia had its equivalent rights stripped away by the Bourbon dynasty in the eighteenth century. More concerted efforts at centralisation in the nineteenth century resulted in the abolition of the *fueros* in 1876, triggering the emergence of Basque nationalism in the first decades of the twentieth century. In the final months of the Second Republic the Partido Nacionalista Vasco (PNV) managed to pass a Basque Statute of Autonomy which would have allowed three Basque provinces—Araba, Gipuzkoa, and Bizkaia—to form an autonomous government. But the onset of the Civil War erased this achievement. From now on Franco's regime would severely repress the Basque people; it was to Gernika in Bizkaia that Franco directed Hitler's Condor Legion of bombers in 1937. The PNV was forced into exile abroad (Tahmassian 2012, pp. 65–8). The Basque language, Euskara, was banned in all educational institutions, and Basque cultural expressions prohibited. During his *caudillaje*, Franco would declare a total of twelve states of exception, half of which were targeted specifically at the Basque provinces. These allowed the regime to detain people for up to seventy-two hours without either notifying their family or bringing formal charges

Imagining the political past 81

(Muro 2008, pp. 91–93). Generalising repression in this way affected not just militant Basque nationalists but the entire Basque population, a clear internal enemy against which the regime came to define itself (Tahmassian 2012).

After Franco's death in 1975 repression against the Basques continued. Armed police charged on strikers in Vitoria-Gasteiz in 1976, shooting dead five labourers and injuring 150 others. Two more people were killed and many wounded just a few months later in Montejurra, when police ordered an extreme-right militia to charge on a crowd. As Lena Tahmassian points out, the figure ultimately responsible for these deaths was Manuel Fraga. Fraga had once been Minister of Information and Tourism under Franco but now, following Franco's death, he took up the post of Second Deputy Prime Minister and Minister of the Interior. With a degree in political law and economics, and a professorship in theory of the state and constitutional law at Madrid's Complutense University, Fraga was not just familiar with the Schmittian legal theory advanced by Francisco Javier Conde and Luis Legaz Lacambra; he was, in Tahmassian's words, a "disciple" of these thinkers (Tahmassian 2012, p. 72). One of Fraga's contemporaries, the exiled Spanish writer and later PSOE culture minister Jorge Semprún, went further, referring to Fraga as a "disciple of Carl Schmitt". It was Fraga who praised Schmitt as Spain's "buen amigo y maestro" (Müller 2003 p. 134, n6), and his publications frequently refer to the German jurist. It was also Fraga who in 1976 founded the Alianza Popular (People's Alliance), the party that some years later evolved into the PP.

When the PSOE won the 1982 elections they hoped that ETA, no longer faced with the Francoist regime that had set back Basque ambitions, but with a democratically-elected government, would cease all terrorist activity (Woodworth 2001, p. 408). But exactly a week later, on 4 November 1982, ETA assassinated General Victor Lago Román, head of one of the most powerful divisions in the Spanish army. From 1983 until 1987 the Grupos Antiterroristas de Liberación (GAL) operated under the PSOE, co-ordinated by officials from the Ministry of the Interior. These "death squads" carried out much of their activity across the border in the French Basque provinces, but they were also responsible for assassinations, torture and kidnappings in Spain. In 1983, following the GAL's murder of twenty-three year old Ramón Oñederra in the French town of Bayonne, the newspaper *El País*—usually supportive of the new Socialist government—wrote that:

> Some people recently arrived in public office seem, on occasions, to be infected with the sickness of "reasons of State". For these arrogant discoverers of the intestines of Leviathan, the defenders of

82   *Imagining the political past*

constitutional guarantees and human rights are … ridiculous puritans, ignorant of the secret codes of public life.

(Quoted in Woodworth 2001, p. 185)

The GAL's activity did little if anything to diminish ETA's potency: in the year before the GAL was established, ETA assassinated forty-four people; in the years during its operation, they continued to kill on average forty people per year (Woodworth 2001, p. 412).

It was a young investigating magistrate at Spain's central court, Baltasar Garzón, whose work finally traced a path from the GAL to the very top of the PSOE. In 1988 Minister of the Interior José Barrionuevo, who had been in the post since the Socialists came to power in 1982, obstructed the court's requests for information about a set of "reserved" government funds employed for unspecified purposes. Garzón had good reason to believe that these funds had been funnelled to a Spanish policeman suspected of paying mercenaries for operations in the Basque country—but Barrionuevo refused to give details about their use (Woodworth 2001, pp. 200–212). It was not so hard to deduce, according to an *El País* editorial, that Barrionuevo was acting not on his own initiative but by order of the head of the government. *El País* was quick to interpret the PSOE's obfuscation in Schmittian terms. Its editorial on 29 June 1988 concluded that "The government's attitude reveals that the principle of legality, established in the Constitution, applies for all citizens, except for the police, who are paradoxically permitted to violate the law in the name of the law". In 1994 José Barrionuevo was convicted of funding and directing GAL's activities following Garzón's investigation. In 1995 Garzón asked the Supreme Court to consider charging then Prime Minister Felipe González with having helped orchestrate the GAL (p. 211). It was Garzón who would later lead attempts to investigate crimes committed by the Franco regime against its opponents.

Following these revelations, which seem likely to have coloured Iglesias' and Errejón's early memories of national politics, the PSOE's war against ETA served for some as a symbol of their continuity with Franco's regime. Rather than the favoured PSOE narrative of leftist politics having finally come to maturity with the 1982–96 government, it became easier to slot the mainstream left into a different and much less flattering story. According to this framing, the left of the modern PSOE could trace its ancestry not to the Republican governments of 1873 or 1931, but rather to the left erected as a smokescreen by fundamentally anti-democratic regimes to mask their true nature. It was, in other words, the descendant of the late-nineteenth-century Liberal Party led by Práxedes Mateo Sagasta, which simply alternated in government with the Conservative Party according to a system designed by Conservative leader Antonio Cánovas. Elections under

Imagining the political past 83

the *turno pacífico* (peaceful turn), as the system was called, were held after the King had already chosen the Government, and were rigged well in advance. All other parties were excluded. The system was dubbed *pacífico* because it was designed to prevent a repeat of the violence that had characterised Spanish politics over the previous century. Democracy was sacrificed in the name of stability, even though what stability was achieved collapsed after the First World War, giving way to the military coup and subsequent dictatorship of Primo Rivera in 1923. It is not too difficult to see how, for leftist students of political history like Iglesias and Errejón, the PSOE might have seemed like Sagasta's party resurrected, a party of the left that would sooner settle for a sham democracy than risk having to fight for the real thing. After all, Iglesias tells us, the majority of the PSOE collaborated with Rivera's dictatorship (Iglesias 2015a, p. 80). War had continually been used as an excuse for curtailing democratic reforms throughout Spanish history, including by the left. And yet war had broken out despite this curtailment.

If the promise of a European future had provided a distraction from this emerging historical narrative in the early 2000s, by the end of the decade its ability to allure had weakened (cf. Torreblanca 2015, p. 136). The financial crisis of 2008 brought with it demands by the German-led Troika to rein in public spending. For those who had come to associate faith in Europe's benevolence with Spanish politicians liable to turn their backs on ordinary Spaniards, historical precedents came easily enough to mind. Gone was the new benevolent and inclusive Europe that wanted only what was in Spain's best interest; back had come the Franco-German Europe of Napoleon, of Hitler, and of the allied powers that refused to give military assistance to the Republican government of 1936 when it was overthrown by Franco's uprising. As the public record in Spain had turned more decisively in the 1990s and 2000s towards blaming Franco's actions for the Civil War, so the neutrality of the allies in the Spanish conflict had begun to seem morally reprehensible. Western European countries such as France and the United Kingdom could no longer pretend to be long-term friends of democracy—any more than could the sham left. European politics was not, and never had been, an idealist politics driven by democratic values; it was a realist politics driven by self-interest. In mid-2012 the German Chancellor Angela Merkel received a letter from the ARMH. It was a request that Germany pay reparations for the damage caused in Spain between 1936 and 1939 by the Condor Legion's bombs (Treglown 2014, p. 276).

These three narratives—of the sham left, of the realism of European politics, and of an unattainable stability time and again being prioritised over democracy—were brought together in mid-2011 when, in response to German-led pressure, the PSOE government introduced a reform that would radically curtail public spending. This "express" reform, the result of

84 *Imagining the political past*

a pact struck with the PP, made it a constitutional obligation for all state administrations to balance their budgets. For Podemos' leaders the pact embodied everything that was wrong with Spain's post-1978 version of liberal democracy. Following in the tradition of twentieth-century international relations as they saw it, Europe had begun to look once again not like Spain's saviour but its jailor. The PSOE, which under Zapatero had subscribed to "Civic Republicanism", was revealed as the party of an elite prepared to sacrifice its democratic ideals in the name of liberal harmony— just as it had during the Transition (Errejón 2011c, p. 70). And with the rise of right-wing populism in the rest of Europe in direct response to the Troika-imposed reforms, the lie was given to the idea that stability might result from such denials of democratic process.

History for Podemos

There can be little doubt that the Podemos leaders imagine themselves as continuing the political tradition of the Republican left of 1931. While their campaigning rhetoric identifies the political enemy as the neoliberal elites within and without Spain, it is not difficult to trace the direct connections in their thought between these elites and Franco's fascism. Against this conservative-liberal antagonist, Podemos demand "a return to the republican values of public virtue and social justice" (Iglesias quoted in Rivero 2015, p. 144). During a discussion of how Spanish cinema might come closer to political truth than it has managed to do so far, Iglesias imagines a film about the Madrid Defence Council, which took over when:

> … the government of the Republic had fled to Valencia and where power, extremely dispersed, was in the hands of leading socialist politicians, anarchists and communists who weren't yet 25 years old, and workers' organisations. In that Madrid where the volunteers of the International Brigades arrived, bombed by the Condor Legion and crawling with fifth-columnists, power was in the hands of the most humble, of those always forgotten by history, in a show of force by the armed democratic resistance faced with a fascism that nowhere in the world had ever known.
>
> (Iglesias 2014a, p. 41)

It was during the Madrid Defence Council's brief existence during the Civil War that public virtue and social justice were most dramatically pitted against their opposites, and as such it is the Civil War that, for Iglesias, "represents an extraordinary source of liberatory political imaginaries, perfectly serviceable for the fight for democratic meanings in the political present" (Iglesias 2014a, p. 42).

Imagining the political past 85

Now that the foundations supporting the Pact of Forgetting have almost entirely disintegrated, the story the Podemos leaders can tell themselves about the Spanish left is fundamentally different from the narrative their parents could construct. But so, consequently, is the story they can tell themselves about the history of Spanish politics itself. No longer should the Civil War be seen as an unfortunate "meteorological event", the result of an exceptional weather pattern following which normal conditions of calm politics were restored. Nor, for that matter, can post-Transition politics be seen as the liberal, consensus-based activity that it purported to be: even though political agreements between left and right during this period might not have appeared as coerced, coercion was nonetheless their pre-condition. The coercion of fact and the coercion of historical memory that resulted were both underpinned by physical force. In this light, events such as the attempted coup of February 1981 have come to seem to the Podemos leaders not as exceptional intrusions that invade an ordered citadel of politics from a chaotic and violent Hobbesian beyond. Instead, such events were the very condition of post-Transition politics, because by ensuring that civil war seemed to the Spanish population like an ever-present possibility, they weakened the left, preventing any moves to "de-Francoise" the police force, to give greater autonomy to the regions, or to recognise democrats who had fought in the Civil War (Iglesias 2015a, pp. 148–9). Stripped of its veil of forgetting, it becomes difficult to see the history of Spanish politics as the history of the ordered citadel on the hill, occasionally threatened by banished and base human passion. Unveiled, Spanish history seems to vindicate Schmitt's view that the situation of exceptionality is not outside the normal juridical order at all, but rather is its very condition.

Thus Iglesias begins his retelling of Spanish history with the military coup against the first Spanish Republic (1873–74), establishing from the outset his view that all political order is founded on violence. During the revolutionary period that had begun in 1868, elites had seen democracy threaten their interests; this, in Iglesias' view, was what triggered the coup (Iglesias 2015a, p. 60). The stability that followed depended on this violent overthrow of the Republican government for its longevity, because it allowed Cánovas to persuade the liberals to agree to the mock-democracy of the *turno pacífico*. The popular political will had been suppressed, ultimately by violence (p. 60). It was the threat of violence that suppressed pluralism when in 1906 a law was passed that put prosecution for offending the unity of the country, its flag or its army under military jurisdiction (p. 66). It was the threat of violence that lay behind the success of the "Bolshevik myth" which, by painting early 1920s Spanish Bolshevism as part of that conspiracy of international Judaism that had engineered the Russian revolution, brought dictator Primo de Rivera to power in 1923 (p. 76).

86 *Imagining the political past*

Franco's coup against the Second Republic in 1936 was nothing outside the norm for Spanish politics, nor was the 1981 *Tejerazo*. All political order, Iglesias tells his readers, is founded on violence; violence is the foundation of politics (p. 38).

It has not been hard for the Podemos intellectuals to extend this view of Spanish politics to the present. Exceptional decisions about who should be considered friends and who should be considered enemies continue, as they see it, to infect Spanish politics to its core. The ruling Partido Popular's military action against ETA in recent years is described by Iglesias, in what is surely an implicit reference to Schmitt, as "based in exceptionality" (Iglesias 2015a, p. 36). Their enmity towards the Basque terrorists structured the PP's reaction to the March 2004 bombings of trains at Madrid's Atocha station in which 192 people were killed. The government blamed ETA for the attacks in the hours that followed; they also made the unprecedented move of pushing the UN Security Council to make a statement blaming ETA (Rivero 2015, pp. 62–3). Even after the security forces indicated that their principal line of investigation had nothing to do with ETA, the Government persisted with its accusation, and two days later the PP's leader, Mariano Rajoy (currently Spain's Prime Minister), declared that he had "the moral conviction that it was ETA" (p. 68). But as it turned out—and as many believed it would turn out—it was not ETA, but al-Qa'ida affiliates who were responsible. During the day of uncertainty that followed the attack, which happened to be the day preceding the 2004 general election, it was someone at the Complutense University—where most of Podemos' present core of leaders were either working or studying at the time—who sent what became a famous, widely-relayed text message calling for people to protest in front of the PP headquarters (cf. Iglesias 2008, p. 450).

A distortion of history?

Even Podemos' political opponents concede that Spain's democratic institutions have suffered something of a legitimacy crisis in recent years. Both Lassalle and Maravall recognise that corruption scandals damaged the image of the established political parties. But whereas Iglesias and Errejón depict these scandals as only the most recent symptoms of a deep sickness that set in after Franco's death, Lassalle and Maravall both diagnose a recently-contracted infection, for which each offers their own reformist cure. In Lassalle's view the infection was caused by global influences that have affected many countries other than Spain; for Maravall the infection came from within the patient's own body. What they agree on, though, is that far from being part of the solution, Podemos is itself a symptom of the real illness.

Imagining the political past 87

Maravall sees Spain's current affliction as a "crisis of social democracy" shared by all the longest-established democracies in Europe, where traditional parties of the left and right are being threatened by "a xenophobic and reactionary populism" (Maravall 2013c). The causes of this crisis cannot be traced back to the 1978 constitution, because until quite recently—at least until the end of the PSOE Government in which Maravall himself served—Spain's politics were characterised by tolerance and a system that worked for those at the top, the bottom, the centre and the periphery of society alike (Maravall 2013a, p. 15). The Transition also succeeded in maintaining Spain's geographic integrity; rather than suppressing those "nationalist identities that had contributed to three civil wars in modern times", the institutions it established managed to "channel" them by protecting the interests of minorities against threat from majorities. What made this possible was nothing less than a "vast" decentralisation of power (Maravall 2016, p. 39; Maravall 2013a, p. 60).

Things only started to go wrong at some point after the 1980s. The 1978 Constitution had laid down all the conditions for democracy to function as it should, stating that parties' "internal structure and functioning must be democratic" (Maravall 2013b; Maravall 2013a, pp. 52–3). But in time parties began to shut themselves off from citizens, organising bureaucratically along geographical lines. As attachments between people and parties weakened—attachments which, in Maravall's view, had until then kept voters well-informed about politics—a space eventually opened up for a new noxious strain of party strategy. "Transversal themes" were now required to attract the free-floating voter no longer held in place by a particular ideology (Maravall 2013a, p. 34). And what theme could be more transversal—more capable of its significance being widely and immediately understood—than the personal inadequacy of particular political leaders? In practice transversal themes translated into *ad hominem* attacks, which came to characterise Spanish political rhetoric in the 2000s.

Unsurprisingly, Maravall blames this debasement of national politics on the PP. According to him, it was Mariano Rajoy who first dragged politics down to this level when he accused Zapatero of being complicit in ETA's terrorism and thus partly responsible for "breaking up Spain" (Maravall 2013a, p. 36). Rajoy's assault was part of a strategy of "extreme tension" underpinned by the principle that the ends justify the means, whatever they might be. Once it had committed to this strategy, the PP was condemned to sustain its "apocalyptic tone", its "dialectic of the enemy in place of that of the adversary" (Maravall 2007). Negative campaigns became the new norm (Maravall 2013a, p. 19), enabling parties to find electoral success despite unprecedentedly low levels of support.

88 *Imagining the political past*

If we are to understand the "xenophobic and reactionary" populism currently afflicting Spain, we must, Maravall implies, do so with an eye on this historical background. When Podemos sets the *casta* against the people, they are simply replicating a strategy first deployed by the PP a decade earlier. And when the PP embarked on this strategy in 2004, they themselves had imported it directly from the US where it was designed by Karl Rove and the neoconservatives (Maravall 2007). Spain's current problems may have their origins in the collapse of Transition-era democratic party structures; but without the imported strategy of "extreme tension" they may not have reached such a critical state. Podemos, Maravall's account implies, is nothing but the latest symptom of a disease that is at least partly foreign in origin. It is this disease—which rots political parties' democratic structure—and not the shortcomings of the Transition that explains Spain's recent troubles.

José María Lassalle similarly draws his readers' attention away from any flaws in the Transition to focus partly on exogenous sources of infection. In a recent book entitled *Contra el Populismo* (*Against Populism*), Lassalle identifies Podemos as just one variant of a recent global populist virus whose other strains include Donald Trump and various right-wing European parties: "We are up against a universal phenomenon that has to do with global historic factors that question inherited political certainties" (Lassalle 2017, 142/1008; 169/1008). From this perspective the main proximate cause of Spain's, and indeed the entire West's, current problems is not some domestic constitutional deficiency but rather the 2008 global financial crisis, just as the "fanatical violence" of the 1930s and 1940s was precipitated by the 1929 Wall Street Crash. Economic collapse has severely undermined faith that progress will inevitably result from rationality. The middle classes fear they will be proletarianised—that they have been cheated out of the future they were promised (360–375/1008). Now, as in the 1930s, the violence and irrationality repressed by the enlightenment are being set free as a kind of "collective neurosis of fear and resentment" grips the West's psyche (188–193 & 360–365/1008). The result is populism.

In Lassalle's pan-national story, the events of 11 September 2001 (9/11) were the initial trigger for this contemporary neurosis. Since the twin towers of the World Trade Center collapsed it has been easier to see democracy as an inherently flawed construction unable to withstand events that make the world ungovernable (214/1008). Generalised fears about the inability of "deliberative representation" to deal with such *global* events have generated a desire for strong leaders unconstrained by the usual rules. Lassalle draws a direct line between the neoconservative Bush administration's military reaction to 9/11 and contemporary populism's Schmittian decisionism (232/1008); out of impatience both "abolish the chronological dimension of rational deliberation" in favour of decision-making

Imagining the political past 89

devoid of thought (219/1008). But these two political movements are not just intellectual doppelgängers; one sired the other. When the US neo-conservatives unleashed a form of ideological warfare in support of their programme, this also infected the European media, which filled with denunciations based on conspiracy theories (285–295/1008). This laid an infrastructure of suspicion capable of supporting a populist surge a decade later (439/1008).

By publishing a book analysing populism as a global phenomenon with global causes, Lassalle is partly trying to supplant Podemos' own narrative focus on domestic problems. Under Lassalle's gaze, Podemos' Schmittian truths become irrational sociological effects rather than objective facts able to serve as the starting point for a new kind of politics. If it is problems of global significance such as 9/11 and the 2008 financial crisis that have fomented irrational dissatisfaction with democracy as it currently exists, then we should dismiss Podemos' own claims about the regime of 1978— the most damaging of which, in Lassalle's view, is the suggestion that the constitution ensured that those who won the Civil War did not emerge as losers from the restoration of democracy (126/1008). These claims are merely part of the fog of suspicion that both left- and right-wing populism alike tactically unleash on society in order to "besiege" established institutions (214/1008); they are little more than a pretext for advancing a form of "low-intensity totalitarianism" (56/1008). Though "society's belief in the foundational story of Spanish democracy" has been undermined by this "anti-political siege" (131/1008), it is a siege with little foundation in truth. Accusations of corruption levelled at domestic elites are nothing but "an excuse that populism uses ... as part of the story that questions the legitimacy of representative theory and the foundations of liberal democracy" (158/1008). Podemos' story about the "regime of 1978" may have found some success in Spain, but it is a dangerous ruse—the product of a psychological sickness afflicting the mind of Western civilisation as a whole.

Since both Maravall and Lassalle dismiss Podemos' discourse as part of a cynical strategy descended from US neoconservatism, their books do not dignify it by engaging directly with its leaders' historical claims about the Transition. This task is left to academics such as Alberto Reig Tapia, a Spanish political historian who has previously written about the right-wing neo-*franquistas*' attempts to obscure history. Reig Tapia acknowledges that the Transition had its problems, but he too dismisses much of Iglesias' and Errejón's retelling of Spanish history.

While it is true, in Reig Tapia's view, that the first attempts at reform from within Franco's regime were "manifestly conservative and suggested a more or less camouflaged continuism", the 1977 elections incontrovertibly set in motion a change of regime. To suggest that representatives elected that

90 *Imagining the political past*

year were silenced or threatened by the military is "completely fallacious", as records of debates at the time clearly demonstrate (Reig Tapia 2016, p. 100). Reig Tapia gives two examples selected to prove that force did not dictate the Transition's outcomes. Firstly, the military's express desires were twice disregarded by elected politicians, once when then Prime Minister Adolfo Suárez legalised the Partido Comunista de España (PCE—Communist Party of Spain) and again when the new Constitution recognised the autonomy of different "historic nationalities" within Spain (p. 102). Secondly, Suárez directly faced down a threat from the military in 1977 when he was confronted by a *franquista* lieutenant-general who warned him he could face a "legitimate" coup d'état if he did not reverse the legalisation of the Comisiones Obreras, a largely Communist workers' union. Suárez retorted by reminding the lieutenant-general that the death penalty for high treason remained part of the Code of Military Justice (p. 103).

The Transition, Reig Tapia maintains, was fundamentally a success. Though it was not a complete "rupture" that consigned every element of Franco's regime to the past, it was nonetheless a "rupturist reform" (Reig Tapia 2016, p. 95) that established genuinely democratic institutions. This is what "the majority of studies of this period"—including Juan Linz' seminal account, as we have seen—have concluded (p. 95). To suggest otherwise is to dismiss all the evidence to the contrary, perhaps most obvious among which is the fact that Spain has experienced "30 years of uninterrupted political and social development" in which "all kinds of political alternative" have been able to emerge and contest elections (p. 107). On this Reig Tapia is aligned with the dominant discourse in the Spanish parliament which, in Javier Franzé's translation, holds that the decades since 1978 have constituted "the period of our history during which there was the greatest freedom, prosperity and democracy" (Franzé 2018, p. 54). For Reig Tapia, the stories that the Podemos leaders and their like tell, in which the Transition represents the "original sin" responsible for all Spain's current problems (Reig Tapia 2016, p. 94), are part of a classic Freudian—and therefore, implicitly, irrational—strategy employed by a rebel teenager confronting his father. Rather than examining how they themselves may be complicit in producing the problems that afflict them, this new generation project all that is negative onto their parents' actions (p. 108).

When Linz and Stepan contrasted the constitutional processes of post-Franco Spain and Weimar Germany in 1996, the Spanish Government was, in the authors' own words, "in the midst of a serious crisis unrelated to the transition" (Reig Tapia 2016, p. 107). High-ranking PSOE ministers' complicity in the murder of ETA militants was beginning to come to light; the ensuing scandal would contribute to the party's defeat in general elections the following year. Linz and Stepan's dissociation of this crisis from

Imagining the political past 91

the Transition was possible partly because it concerned a PSOE government, and the PSOE government had become inextricably associated with what "broad scholarly consensus" held to be democracy's consolidation: the Socialists' election in October 1982. If the start of Spain's political present is dated back not to 1978 but to 1982, then the story told about contemporary Spanish political institutions begins with their passing the ultimate democratic test. In this version of the present, any subsequent deficit of democracy cannot be blamed on institutional foundations; it must be traced back to the irresponsibility of particular parties or individuals.

When Lassalle and Maravall tell their own histories of the present, they follow in Linz' canonical footsteps. Lassalle's primary concern is the evolution of liberalism. When he slices up the political present into four acts, as though describing a stage performance in which liberalism is the major player, none of these starts in 1978. His first period begins with Franco's death in 1975 and lasts until the socialists' election in 1982 (Lassalle 2016). Maravall's primary concern is the evolution not of liberalism but of social democracy. His present begins with Felipe González' call shortly after the 1981 attempted coup for a "deepening of democracy" and the PSOE's subsequent election in 1982 (Maravall 2013a, p. 20).

By choosing to date the political present back to 1978 instead, Podemos conversely begin their story with instability. The effect may be, as Duncan Wheeler suggests, to "[distract] attention away from the 1980s, a less-contested decade that offers fewer mitigating circumstances for Spanish political elites and the general public alike" (Wheeler 2017, p. 459). When you begin your history of the present with the signing of the Constitution rather than the consolidation of democracy—when you refer constantly to the "regime of '78"—it may seem as though the long decade between the PSOE's election in 1982 and their downfall in the mid-1990s was the real aberration in 40 years of otherwise non-progressive and undemocratic government. Political perspective can be altered profoundly by periodisation.

Schmitt as political realist

It is possible to see a softening in the Podemos intellectuals' stance towards the Transition as they have become more closely entangled with the political institutions it helped establish. The focus of their blame has arguably shifted from the 1978 pacts to the political elite's management of the 2008 financial crisis (Franzé 2018, p. 60), bringing them closer to the critiques of social democrats like Maravall (see Franzé 2018, p. 64). And now that they themselves are deputies in the Spanish parliament, their pejorative references to *la casta* have been displaced by less generalising allusions to "*la trama*", a web or conspiracy of politicians and ex-politicians, business

92 *Imagining the political past*

leaders, media executives and bankers who constitute a corrupt and self-enriching oligarchy (García de Blas 2017; López de Miguel 2017). But Iglesias and Errejón's general conception of politics, in which enmity and the possibility of violence form the substrate on which normal politics sits, appears to have been enduringly Schmittian; in their view this conception is simply what being a realist about Spanish politics requires.

It was a vision of politics inspired by "accursed writers" including Schmitt that Iglesias brought to his 2013 analysis of cinema, *Machiavelli Before the Big Screen*. While others would consider Schmitt and his political-theoretical predecessors like the Marquis de Sade, Hobbes, and Lenin to be "too dangerous" an influence, Iglesias, all of whose work is coloured by Spanish history, promised his readers "a homage to dangerous political friendships" with writers from this bleak tradition (Iglesias 2013a, p. 9). A quote from Weber introduces a chapter that articulates the political truth of Lars von Trier's film *Dogville* through Giorgio Agamben's neo-Schmittian theory: "whoever does politics makes a pact with the diabolical forces that lie in wait for all power" (Weber quoted in Iglesias 2013a, p. 51). "Political truth", Iglesias clarifies, is "always unilateral"; it is imposed by victors on the vanquished in "moments of exceptionality", and a "predominant ideology of compromise" only obscures this fact (p. 57). Doing real politics requires us to shoulder the "immense responsibility" that accompanies unilateral action backed by violence; it is because they recognise this that true Leninists and conservative politicians have something in common (p. 59). "[O]nly violence has the power to establish that which we call universal values", Iglesias tells his readers; "horror, as Robespierre knew, is often the truth of politics" (p. 79). If it takes dangerous political friendships with thinkers like Schmitt to recognise this, so be it. Perverse though it may seem, Iglesias implies that there may be no other way of restoring public virtue and social justice in Spain.

Applied to Spain, Schmitt's lesson is that there always will be, as there always has been, a group cast in the role that ETA currently occupies: a branch of humanity without political rights, what Giorgio Agamben calls *homo sacer* (Iglesias 2013a, pp. 55–6). Once this is acknowledged, the important question is no longer whether we should have a politics that permits such enmity, because from the perspective of Schmittian realism such a question makes no sense. The Basque conflict has, in Errejón's words, been the "constitutive outside" of Spanish politics, without which it could not have existed. So the important question becomes who has the power to decide the identity of the outcasts, and who is able to hold onto that power. "[T]he difference between a terrorist and a patriot", Iglesias writes, "the difference between presidents who pass into history and those who die hanged, is simply the difference between victory and defeat" (p. 141).

Imagining the political past 93

It is in part precisely because of the prior influence of Schmitt's decisionism itself that Spain's recent political history has come to look so Schmittian to Iglesias and Errejón. At least until the late 1970s Schmitt's political theory was helping to shape Spanish political reality in its own image; his vision of politics was being partially *performed* by the political Right (see Callon 2008)—especially through its response to ETA. The vehicle for this instance of political-theoretical performativity was the Instituto de Estudios Políticos, which was infused with Schmitt's ideas throughout its existence. Schmitt himself was made an honorary member in 1962. His student Francisco Javier Conde was its director between 1949 and 1956; Luis Legaz Lacambra from 1970 to 1974. Midway between the two, Manuel Fraga—the man ultimately responsible both for repressing the Basques in the immediate post-Transition era and for the PP's existence—briefly held its reins between 1960 and 1961. The Instituto still exists today, though under a different name: the Centro de Estudios Políticos y Constitucionales.

In accounting for the Podemos leaders' appropriation of Schmitt, we must not forget that they are public intellectuals as well as politicians. Though you are unlikely to find Iglesias or Errejón referencing theorists such as Schmitt on mainstream TV talk shows or at party rallies, the academic impulse to reveal what they see as the truth clearly asserts itself even under these extramural conditions. Among the political injustices Podemos wishes to address—perhaps the greatest of these political injustices—is the injustice of distorted historical memory, and the only way to combat this injustice is through political truth-telling, no matter how uncomfortable it might be. "Spain has a debt to people who gave everything to defend liberty", in Errejón's words, and this debt must be repaid through the construction of a "democratic memory" (Gómez 2016).

Article 261 of Podemos' 2016 manifesto, entitled "Memory, truth and justice", dwells on the need for this intellectual corrective. "Starting from the double premise that memory is a human right and that in Spain a true public policy of memory has still not been implemented", Podemos outline a number of specific steps they would take were they elected. One would remove or "resignify" symbols or monuments that celebrate Franco's uprising or his regime. Another would seek to restore a "plural, collective and democratic" memory in the educational system, in the training of civil servants and through the media. "Institutional mechanisms" would be established to "clarify and divulge" the truth; a detailed map of communal graves would be created, paving the way for a comprehensive plan for exhuming the remains they hold. A ministry would be created with its own secretary of state responsible for ensuring access to justice for the victims of *franquismo* (Unidos Podemos 2016). Spain's truth is, in the eyes of Podemos' leaders, one of ineradicable enmity.

94　*Imagining the political past*

Excising any remnants of Schmitt's thought from their rhetoric perhaps would have been politically expedient for the sake of electoral success, but by doing so Iglesias and Errejón would have compromised their ability to correct the injustice of distorted collective memory. For these sons of leftist activists Schmitt's political theory helps to lay down a direct path to the truth of Spanish history, which has been obscured by even the best-intentioned producers of popular culture. Now, through their political speech, Iglesias and Errejón can reach a mass audience that as academics they would never have reached. Iglesias laments that the only people who sell books about the Civil War are authors whose work no historian considers to have academic merit. Serious academics are not read on this topic because they lack sufficient media presence (Torreblanca 2015, p. 99). But as populist politicians Iglesias and Errejón have become producers of popular culture themselves; they are no longer confined to critiquing others for failing to tell what they see as the Schmittian truth of Spanish political history, and can tell this truth themselves.

Nostalgia

It is apparently not just its ability to lay bare the truth of Spanish history, though, that attracted Iglesias and Errejón to Schmitt's vision; nostalgia also seems to be at work here. As Paul Preston notes, the Civil War has become a focus for new generations in search of the "idealism and sacrifice so singularly absent from modern politics" (Preston 2006, p. 5). Iglesias writes approvingly of the "utopian excess" present in struggles of the past that "can nourish our struggles today" (Iglesias 2015a, p. 112), and it is this utopian excess that he and Errejón seem to feel their generation has been cheated out of. In an interview Errejón concedes that what motivates him is a desire to "reconstruct community again and to feel part of something" (Gómez 2016). Where one's major historical reference for feeling "part of something" is the "utopian excess" that animated a war—that of the Madrid Defence Council in that heady half-year between November 1936 and April 1937—perhaps it should come as no surprise that Schmitt's political theory is appealing.

Memories of this kind allow their bearers to understand themselves as part of a lineage of fighters taking up a struggle that was never abandoned by their parents and grandparents. Errejón is dismissive of those who would deny his generation their own adventures:

> [The generation of '78's] story would go: 'We made history and that was the time of great epics. Now that's already been done. Go back home. Study a lot, get rich, and have fun on the weekends. The time of collective feats is over'. 'We did the best we could'. 'We've already

Imagining the political past 95

been heroes, we ran in front of Franco's police. The time of collective hopes is over'. And yet, no society can stay healthy without communal goals and hopes.

(Errejón and Mouffe 2016, p. 35)

Errejón and his contemporaries, especially those equipped "with memory", will not be denied their own opportunity to run "without fear" before the metaphorical infantry of an opposing force.

In her book on the causes of the war that defined Schmitt's youth, Margaret MacMillan registers the significance of such feelings. In the years leading up to 1914, life had become

easier, especially for the middle and lower classes, but it was not necessarily more interesting. Far off colonial wars, while the publics followed them with interest, did not fully satisfy longings for glory and great deeds. The spread of literacy as well as the new mass newspapers, historical novels, thrillers, pulp fiction, or Westerns showed alternative, more enthralling worlds. To the dismay of anti-war liberals, war was glamorous. As one said in Britain, 'Long immunity from the realities of warfare has blunted our imaginations. We love excitement not a whit less than the Latin races; our lives are dull; a victory is a thing the meanest of us can understand.' The younger generations wondered, as they sometimes do today, how they would match up in great conflicts. In Germany, young men who had done their military service felt inferior to their elders who had fought in the wars of unification and longed for a chance to prove themselves.

(MacMillan 2014, p. 265)

So while "Europeans were preparing themselves psychologically for war before 1914; some also found the prospect exciting" (MacMillan 2014, p. 264). Schmitt was no exception: "When I see the masses of soldiers marching past and think that one day I shall be one of them", Schmitt wrote in August 1914, "I feel a strong excitement, even elation [*Erhebung*]"— although he also confessed a month later that he was "often afraid of the horrible war" (quoted in Mehring 2014, p. 55).

Neoliberalism is, of course, problematic for Iglesias and Errejón because of the economic inequality it promotes. But as for the anti-liberals of Schmitt's day, it is also problematic simply because it is *boring*. By continuing to promote the liberal ideal of "solitary individuals who make decisions dispassionately ... from the comfort of their own sofas" (Errejón and Mouffe 2016, p. 66), neoliberalism takes all the excitement out of politics. If Errejón believes that the "joy of shared collective forms of

96 *Imagining the political past*

identification" must be rediscovered (p. 66), it is not just because doing so is strategically good for Podemos; it is because such joy is valuable in itself. What Iglesias and Errejón want is to participate in their own political drama of the kind that neoliberalism refuses to permit. The reference to "great epics" is not accidental.

Compounding the desire to make their own time a "time of great epics" are the particular frustrations of academia that the Podemos intellectuals have experienced. "The frustration we felt was enormous", Iglesias confesses; "far from being organic intellectuals ... we were trapped by academic walls which separated us from society and from a left, our own, profoundly debilitated by both infantile and senile illnesses" (Iglesias 2014a, p. 20). Podemos itself resulted from "the preoccupations of a group of frustrated political scientists" (Iglesias 2015a, p. 93). After building up for so many years, it should perhaps be unsurprising that this frustration burst forth clad in a conceptual armour as vital and aggressive as Schmitt's. In the face of dull reality, a political theory that its author originally labelled "realist" to distinguish it from the romanticism of the liberal worldview (Kennedy 2004, p. 19, pp. 51–3) was now being deployed by young Spanish intellectuals to romanticise their lives.

Schmitt's conception of politics promises drama in abundance; what he recommends is a kind of public political theatre. In his words, "the people exist only in the sphere of publicity"—they must be dragged from their parlour seats onto the public stage where together they will perform political theatre in which the stakes are as high as they possibly can be and a "national energy" is released (cf. Schmitt 1985, p. 69, p. 75). No matter if the performance is based on a fiction: as Mussolini said, "we have created a myth, this myth is a belief, a noble enthusiasm; it does not need to be reality, it is a striving and a hope, belief and courage" (pp. 75–76). Recognising the importance of creating dramatic collective fictions was, in Schmitt's view, nothing other than political realism.

Note

1 In this section we try to see Spanish political history through the eyes of Podemos' leaders without passing judgment on their reconstruction of the past. For a sympathetic but not uncritical assessment of Podemos' position that sets this against alternative left-wing narratives, see Wheeler 2017.

References

Aguilar, Paloma. 2007. "Los debates sobre la memoria histórica". *Claves de Razón Práctica*, 172. pp. 64–69.

Imagining the political past 97

Aguilar, Paloma. 2009. "Whatever happened to Francoist socialization? Spaniards' values and patterns of cultural consumption in the post-dictatorial period". *Democratization*, 16:3. pp. 455–484.

Aguilar, Paloma and Leigh A. Payne. 2016. *Revealing New Truths about Spain's Violent Past: Perpetrators' Confessions and Victim Exhumations.* London: Palgrave Macmillan.

Anson, Luis María. 2005. "La lucidez de Mayor Oreja". *La Razón*, 11 April. Available at www.lbouza.net/ESPANA/anson39.htm. Last accessed 27 February 2018.

Boyd, Carolyn P. 2008. "The Politics of History and Memory in Democratic Spain". *Annals of the American Academy of Political and Social Science* 133. pp. 133–148.

Burgen, Stephen. 2016. "Podemos leaders deny Venezuela government funding link claims". *The Guardian*, 6 April.

Cádiz Cortes. 1812. *The Political Constitution of the Spanish Monarchy: Promulgated in Cádiz, the nineteenth day of March.* Available at www.cervantesvirtual. com/servlet/SirveObras/c1812/12159396448091522976624/p0000001.htm #I_1_. Last accessed 27 February 2018.

Callon, Michel. 2008. "What Does It Mean to Say That Economics Is Performative?". In *Do Economists Make Markets? On the Performativity of Economics.* Edited by Donald MacKenzie, Fabian Muniesa and Lucia Siu. Princeton, NJ: Princeton University Press.

Campelo, P. 2010. "'Tarjeta roja' a Rosa Diez en la universidad". *Público.* 21 October. Available at www.publico.es/espana/tarjeta-roja-rosa-diez-universidad. html. Last accessed 27 February 2018.

Cardús i Ros, Salvador. 2000. "Politics and the Invention of Memory. For a Sociology of the Transition to Democracy in Spain". In *Disremembering the Dictatorship.* Edited by Joan Ramon Resina. Amsterdam: Rodopi.

Casanova, Julián and Carlos Gil Andrés. 2014. *Twentieth Century Spain: A History.* Cambridge: Cambridge University Press.

Centro de Investigaciones Sociológicas. 2008. "Memorias de la Guerra Civil y el Franquismo". *Estudio* 2760 (April).

Chicote, Javier. 2016. "Chávez pagó 7 millones de euros para 'crear en España fuerzas políticas bolivarianas'". *ABC España*, 17 April. Available at www.abc.es/ espana/abci-chavez-pago-7-millones-euros-para-crear-espana-fuerzas-politicas-b olivarianas-201604050224_noticia.html. Last accessed 27 February 2018.

Contrapoder. 2006. "Definición política de Contrapoder". *aucontrapoder.wordpress. com.* 26 October. Available at https://aucontrapoder.wordpress.com/2006/ 10/26/definicion-politica-de-contrapoder/. Last accessed 27 February 2018.

Desfor Eldes, Laura. 2010. *Symbol and Ritual in the New Spain: The Transition to Democracy after Franco.* Cambridge: Cambridge University Press.

El País. 1998. "El Gobierno de Aznar asegura que no irá en contra de las decisiones judiciales". 20 October.

Encarnación, Omar. 2014. *Democracy Without Justice in Spain: The Politics of Forgetting.* Philadelphia: University of Pennsylvania Press.

98   *Imagining the political past*

Errejón, Íñigo. 2011c. "Algo habrán hecho bien. Una juventud «sin futuro» pero con estilo". *Juventud sin Futuro*. Barcelona: Icaria.

Errejón, Íñigo and Pablo Iglesias. 2009. "Lo que consiguió el acto de Evo Morales en la Universidad". *Rebelión*. 18 September. Available at www.rebelion.org/noticia.php?id=91665. Last accessed 27 February 2018.

Errejón, Íñigo and Chantal Mouffe. 2016. *Podemos: In the Name of the People*. London: Lawrence & Wishart.

Franzé, Javier. 2018. "The Podemos Discourse: A Journey from Antagonism to Agonism". In *Podemos and the New Political Cycle: Left-Wing Populism and Anti-Establishment Politics*. Edited by Óscar García Agustín and Marco Briziarelli. Cham, Switzerland: Palgrave Macmillan.

García de Blas, Elsa. 2017. "Podemos reemplaza la 'casta' por la 'trama'". *El País*. 13 March.

Gobierno de España. 2004. "Real Decreto 1891/2004, de 10 de septiembre, por el que se crea la Comisión Interministerial para el estudio de la situación de las víctimas de la guerra civil y del franquismo". *Boletín Oficial del Estado*, núm 227. 20 September. Available at www.boe.es/diario_boe/txt.php?id=BOE-A-2004-16360. Last accessed 27 February 2018.

Gómez, Javi. 2016. "Íñigo Errejón: 'Hemos podemizado España y nos hemos manchado de España'". Interview with Íñigo Errejón. *El Mundo: Papel*. 15 May.

Graham, Helen. 2012. *The War and its Shadow: Spain's Civil War in Europe's Long Twentieth Century*. Brighton: Sussex Academic Press.

Gunther, Richard. 2011. "The Spanish Model Revisited". In *The Politics and Memory of Democratic Transition: The Spanish Model*. Edited by Diego Muro and Gregorio Alonso. London: Routledge.

Iglesias, Pablo. 2008. *Multitud y acción colectiva postnacional: un estudio comparado de los desobedientes: de Italia a Madrid (2000–2005)*. Doctoral thesis (unpublished). Faculty of Political Sciences and Sociology, Complutense University of Madrid.

Iglesias, Pablo. 2013a. *Maquiavelo frente a la gran pantalla: cine y política*. Madrid: Ediciones Akal.

Iglesias, Pablo. 2014a. *Disputar la democracia: política para tiempos de crisis*. Madrid: Ediciones Akal.

Iglesias, Pablo. 2015a. *Una nueva Transición: materiales del año del cambio*. Second Edition. Madrid: Ediciones Akal.

Iglesias, Pablo. 2016. "Carta abierta a Íñigo". *20 Minutos*. 12 December. Available at www.20minutos.es/opiniones/pablo-iglesias-carta-abierta-inigo-2909440. Last accessed 27 February 2018.

Jimeno, Roldán. 2017. *Amnesties, Pardons and Transitional Justice: Spain's Pact of Forgetting*. London: Routledge.

Kennedy, Ellen. 2004. *Constitutional Failure: Carl Schmitt in Weimar*. Durham, NC and London: Duke University Press.

Labanyi, Jo. 2000. "History and Hauntology; or, What Does One Do with the Ghosts of the Past? Reflections on Spanish Film and Fiction of the Post-Franco

Imagining the political past 99

Period". In *Disremembering the Dictatorship*. Edited by Joan Ramon Resina. Amsterdam: Rodopi.

Labanyi, Jo. 2007. "Memory and Modernity in Democratic Spain: The Difficulty of Coming to Terms with the Spanish Civil War". *Poetics Today*, 28:1. pp. 89–116.

Lassalle, José María. 2017. *Contra el populismo: Cartografía de un totalitarismo posmoderno*. Digital edition (Amazon Kindle). Barcelona: Penguin Random House.

Linz, Juan J. and Alfred Stepan. 1996. *Problems of Democratic Transition and Consolidation: Southern Europe, South America, and Post-Communist Europe*. Baltimore, MD: The Johns Hopkins University Press.

López de Miguel, Alejandro. 2017. "Cambio de discurso en el nuevo Podemos: de la casta a la trama". *Público*. 5 March.

MacMillan, Margaret. 2014. *The War that Ended Peace: How Europe Abandoned Peace for the First World War*. London: Profile.

Malamud, Carlos. 2003. "Spanish Public Opinion and the Pinochet Case". In *The Pinochet Case: Origins, Progress and Implications*. Edited by Madeleine Davis. London: ILAS, University of London.

Maravall, José María. 2007. "La crispación". *El País*, 7 May.

Maravall, José María. 2013a. *Las Promesas Políticas*. Barcelona: Galaxia Gutenberg.

Maravall, José María. 2013b. "La hostilidad respecto de los partidos". *El País*, 24 February.

Maravall, José María. 2013c. "En el túnel". *El País*, 14 May.

Maravall, José María. 2016. *Demands on Democracy*. Oxford: Oxford University Press.

Martí, José Luis and Philip Pettit. 2010. *A Political Philosophy in Public Life: Civil Republicanism in Zapatero's Spain*. Princeton, NJ: Princeton University Press.

Mehring, Reinhard. 2014. *Carl Schmitt: A Biography*. Translated by Daniel Steuer. Cambridge: Polity Press.

Müller, Jan-Werner. 2003. *A Dangerous Mind: Carl Schmitt in Post-War European Thought*. New Haven, CT: Yale University Press.

Muro, Diego. 2008. *Ethnicity and Violence: The Case of Radical Basque Nationalism*. New York: Routledge.

Núñez Seixas, Xosé M. 2017. "The language(s) of the Spanish nation." In *Metaphors of Spain; Representations of Spanish National Identity in the Twentieth Century*. Edited by Javier Moreno-Luzón and Xosé M. Núñez Seixas. New York: Berghahn.

Phillips, William D., Jr., and Carla Rahn Phillips. 2010. *A Concise History of Spain*. Cambridge: Cambridge University Press.

Preston, Paul. 2006. *The Spanish Civil War: Reaction, Revolution and Revenge*. London: Harper Perennial.

Ramon Resina, Joan. "Short of Memory: the Reclamation of the Past Since the Spanish Transition to Democracy". In *Disremembering the Dictatorship*. Edited by Joan Ramon Resina. Amsterdam: Rodopi.

Reig Tapia, Alberto. 2016. "¿Un nuevo fracaso histórico? La transición a la democracia, el Rey Juan Carlos I y el derecho a decidir". In *Transiciones en el mundo*

100   *Imagining the political past*

contemporáneo. Edited by Alberto Reig Tapia and Josep Sánchez Cervelló. Tarragona/Mexico City: Publicacions Universitat Rovira i Virgili/Universidad Nacional Autónoma de México.

Renshaw, Layla. 2016. *Exhuming Loss: Memory, Materiality and Mass Graves of the Spanish Civil War*. London: Routledge.

Rivero, Jacobo. 2015. *Podemos. Objetivo: asaltar los cielos*. Barcelona: Editorial Planeta.

Schmitt, Carl. 1985. *The Crisis of Parliamentary Democracy*. Translated by Ellen Kennedy. London: The MIT Press.

Schmitt, Carl. 2005. *Political Theology*. Translated by George Schwab. London: University of Chicago Press.

Schmitt, Carl. 2007a. *The Concept of the Political*. Expanded Edition. Translated by George Schwab. London: University of Chicago Press.

Tahmassian, Lena. 2012. "Carl Schmitt and the Basque conflict: from the design of francoism to Spanish democracy". *Journal of Spanish Cultural Studies*, 13:1. pp. 59–81.

Torreblanca, José Ignacio. 2015. *Asaltar los cielos: Podemos o la política después de la crisis*. Second Edition. Barcelona: Penguin Random House.

Treglown, Jeremy. 2014. *Franco's Crypt: Spanish Culture and Memory Since 1936*. London: Chatto & Windus.

Unidos Podemos. 2016. *Programa*. Available at https://lasonrisadeunpais.es/programa/.

Wheeler, Duncan. 2017. "The Generation Game: Javier Cercas, Podemos and the (Im)Possibility of Progressive Politics in Spain". *MLN* 132:2. pp. 441–460.

Woodworth, Paddy. 2001. *Dirty War, Clean Hands: ETA, the GAL and Spanish Democracy*. Cork, Ireland: Cork University Press.

5 Imagining the political future

If Iglesias' and Errejón's historical memory provides adequate material for a Schmittian rendering of Spain's political past, their experiences of politics closer to the present provide more than adequate material for a Schmittian vision of its future. Completed some years before Podemos was founded, their doctoral theses—Iglesias' on conflictive protest in Europe and Errejón's on populism in Bolivia—reveal a series of formative encounters that have become the basis for their political optimism. At this stage Iglesias and Errejón referred only occasionally to Schmitt, recognising the relevance of his thought to aspects of the events they were discussing but not framing their ideas in an entirely Schmittian framework. It is only once the material from each of their theses is combined that a more fully Schmittian reading of the politics of the future falls out.

Iglesias' Thesis

Iglesias' intellectual formation in political science began while studying law in Bologna on an Erasmus exchange. In his thesis he relates how during that year, 1999–2000, he spent most of his time not in his host faculty but in the Faculty of Political Science, in an "occupied and self-governed" classroom (Iglesias 2008, p. 21). Having watched the 1999 Seattle protests around the World Trade Organization conference with interest, in 2000 Iglesias participated in protests against the Organisation for Economic Co-operation and Development in Bologna (p. 259). It was to Italian politics that Iglesias returned in his doctoral thesis, and specifically to Italian political activism that inspired imitations back in Spain (p. 46). As José Ignacio Torreblanca points out though, Iglesias' thesis—a comparative study of the use of civil disobedience by anti-globalisation protesters in Italy and Madrid from 2000–2005—failed to provide him with a blueprint for successful anti-neoliberal politics (Torreblanca 2015, pp. 57–66). Even though Iglesias saw potential in the social movements he studied, he admitted that

102   *Imagining the political future*

their capacity to significantly challenge the political status quo was far from that of movements elsewhere, such as in Latin America (Iglesias 2008, p. 148, p. 505). Still, Iglesias' thesis does give us some sense of how he became comfortable with the idea that force might be a necessary political tool for the left—especially force beyond the law (p. 278)—and also of how he believes that activists like himself become comfortable with this idea in the first place.

From the 1999 Seattle protests onwards, anti-globalisation activists came up against "red zones", which Iglesias describes as "spaces of exceptionality, militarised perimeters" within which activists are not permitted. Since Seattle, "exceptionality has been a permanent political recourse" for democratic-liberal governments against anti-globalisation activism, despite the fact that it requires these governments to renounce their own laws guaranteeing civil and political rights (Iglesias 2008, p. 219). The activists Iglesias studied know first-hand that even in societies that purport to base themselves on law, there is—as Schmitt recognised—power beyond the law, that this power is backed by military force, and that it feeds off opposition to an enemy. One of their most successful tactics is therefore to invade spaces of exceptionality themselves, provoking confrontations with the authorities and contesting their version of order (p. 219). These confrontations not only send a clear political message through the media; they also play the crucial role of consolidating social movements' political identities as they become "mythical-symbolic elements" whose life is extended through songs, novels, documentaries and films (p. 281).

When political activists come to decide which techniques of collective action to employ, "empathy with armed struggle, and also its mythification, are more important than they might seem". Even though the use of force in protest is very different to militarised violence, in Iglesias' view the two registers of force have "a very similar capacity for the production of meaning". So while Italian protesters in the early 2000s rejected violence, they sought to design forms of disruptive collective action that retained the "communicative, propagandistic and identity-forming" capacity of mythified versions of the "partisan antifascist" struggle, of urban guerrilla warfare, and of the left's armed struggle in the 1970s and 1980s. Spanish protesters drew on similar elements of their own country's history, including the Civil War, for the same reason (Iglesias 2008, p. 69). It is worth noting that Errejón, a participant in the Madrid protests, provided "valuable testimony" for the development of Iglesias' analysis of Spanish anti-globalisation activism in this period (p. 67).

Though Iglesias tries to separate violent from non-violent use of force in theory, the fact that one empirically inspired the other suggests the difficulty of doing so in practice. The *tute bianche*—an activist group named

Imagining the political future 103

after the white overalls reminiscent of factory-workers' uniforms in which they protested—went to some lengths to ensure they were equipped with shields, helmets and padded vests in the expectation that they would provoke police violence when they deviated deliberately from routes agreed with the authorities (Iglesias 2008, pp. 238–239). Anti-globalisation activists may not have intended to perpetrate violence, but they intentionally took part in violent clashes—which could in exceptional cases be fatal—for political ends (pp. 243–4). In Geneva, Iglesias tells us, the way in which police chose to manage the 2001 anti-Group of Seven (G7) protests "made urban guerrilla warfare the only possible conflictive relation between protesters and police" (p. 302). In his view the police *expected* people to die.

In detail befitting a legal defence of the protesters, Iglesias recounts the events that led up to the death of activist Carlo Giuliani, who was shot by a *carabiniere* (Iglesias 2008, pp. 323–349). After hours of clashes between police and protesters, the *carabinieri* decided to charge the barricades set up by the *desobedientes*—the "disobedients". Protesters responded by attacking the *carabinieri's* armoured vehicles, which had become isolated because they were unable to manoeuvre properly in Geneva's narrow streets (p. 340). Iglesias suggests that the *carabinieri* knew this was a perilous strategy that might result in deaths—either of protesters or of the armoured vehicles' drivers—and that this escalation was deliberate (p. 348). On the *carabinieri's* second charge, one of their armoured vehicles was first bombarded with stones, making the safe exit of its personnel extremely difficult, and then burned. On the third, Iglesias tells us, *carabinieri* in an armed four-wheel-drive vehicle, isolated and under attack by protesters, shot Giuliani in the face. In Iglesias' view, the abandonment of the *carabinieri* by their colleagues is evidence that the authorities were looking to provoke a deadly encounter; this was the third time they had left one of their vehicles isolated, putting their personnel in grave danger (p. 349). In a subsequent parliamentary inquiry, politicians neglected to view all of the video evidence available—which in Iglesias' opinion demonstrates clearly the *carabinieri's* "tactical intentions"—choosing instead to listen only to oral testimony (p. 322). Iglesias directly accuses the authorities of lying about the events of that day (cf. p. 337).

Iglesias situates the disobedients' actions, which he evidently admires, somewhere between street protest and urban warfare, in a tradition that stretches back to the barricades of the Paris Commune but which also includes the *antifranquista* struggle in Spain (Iglesias 2008, p. 369). The disobedients sought out a space between conventional institutional activity and political violence; their communicative strategy was to "stage" a conflict that would allow them to generate effective political messages through the media in which the authorities are portrayed as needlessly

104 *Imagining the political future*

violent (p. 368, p. 375). In later protests the disobedients would broadcast their conflicts via their own TV channel, "Global TV", which could also be accessed online (p. 396). With time the messages these mediatized actions send will only be amplified by "the mythifying filter of History" (p. 370).

Though the forceful protest tactics that Iglesias analyses involve low levels of violence and are primarily symbolic, they are nonetheless the focus of his work; his thesis examines how, following the Geneva protests, these "conflictive" tactics became part of a modular approach to disobedience, whereby more violent units could be tacked onto mainstream majorities of ordinary protesters. This meant uniting with more traditional forms of social organisation. In the Madrid *barrio* of Lavapiés, where Podemos was born, the Spanish equivalent of the *tute bianche* defended a self-managed social centre against closure in 2001 (Iglesias 2008, p. 402). Two years later, on 23 February 2003, they participated in protests against the Spanish Government's handling of the ecological disaster caused by the spilling of oil from the stricken tanker *MV Prestige* off the Galician coast. Their cause was aided symbolically by the fact that those involved in the clean-up operation, strung out along the Galician beaches, were also wearing overalls for self-protection (p. 410). In a document entitled "Exhuming the axe of war", the *monos blancos* declared that they were going to "attack the heavens once again". Linking these actions to the anti-war protests, they would "defy the military"—"what better day to do this", they asked, "than on February 23rd", the date of the attempted coup fronted by Lieutenant-Colonel Tejero in 1981 (p. 409)?

Ironically it was during the "antibellicose" protests against the Iraq war in March 2003 that the strategies trialled in Italy were imported to Madrid (Iglesias 2008, p.46). On the morning after the USA and its allies, which included Spain, began their invasion of Iraq, students marched from Madrid's main university campuses towards Parliament (p. 417). Thus began days of protests to which a few dozen disobedients, many of whom had taken part in the initial student march, brought along shields and red helmets. Again, in Iglesias' view, it was the authorities who began the violent clashes that took place on 22 March. In a "very dangerous manoeuvre" reminiscent of that of the *carabinieri* in Geneva, riot police cut protesters off from both sides and charged (p. 426). Iglesias describes himself as a "direct witness" to this "unjustifiable" act which sparked hours of violent clashes (pp. 428–9). Several people, including police, were injured (p. 431). The government had, in Iglesias' retelling, "forced extremely violent dynamics" by using riot police to suppress the protests (p. 433). And yet the Izquierda Unida coalition was split between those who supported the protesters and those who called for their prosecution. A few days later some of the disobedients presented Gaspar Llamazares, General

Imagining the political future 105

Co-ordinator of Izquierda Unida, with a rubber bullet fired by the police and one of the helmets they had used to protect themselves, claiming their "right to self-protection faced with police aggression". The presentation happened to take place at Iglesias' own Faculty of Political Sciences at the Complutense, where Llamazares was speaking at a conference (p. 434).

In mid-2003 various experienced activist groups united to form the direct action collective known as Arde Madrid. They were critical of earlier protests that had held back against the Government, and advocated "crossing ... the line of the red zone" into "spaces without rights, without democracy, without rebelliousness"—precisely what Iglesias refers to earlier as places of "exceptionality" (Iglesias 2008, p. 436). "[C]onfronting the enemy" would, Arde Madrid admitted, carry risks, but democracy does not come "as a gift"; it must be "imposed in conflict" (p. 436). Despite their ambitions, however, the Arde Madrid project petered out in Spain, though it would later co-ordinate the attendance of a contingent of Madrid activists at the 2005 Group of Eight (G8) protests in Scotland (p. 437). The last protests Iglesias analyses—the protests that drew on all the disobedients' earlier experiences in Italy and Spain—were those that took place on 13 March 2004 outside the headquarters of the Partido Popular (PP—People's Party) in the days after the Government of José María Aznar falsely accused the Basque separatist group Euskadi Ta Askatasuna (ETA) of orchestrating the attacks on trains at Madrid's Atocha station. Iglesias, who participated, criticises existing accounts of these protests for attributing their power to "civil society" and omitting that they would not have been possible without the conflictive strategies of the disobedients (pp. 450–451). These conflictive strategies allowed the so-called "13-M" protests to be "autonomous with respect to representative democracy"—to "put in question many of its normative foundations" and to challenge the "notion of popular sovereignty represented in parliamentary chambers" as well as "general elections as a mechanism for accessing political power" (p. 452).

It is little wonder that Iglesias found affinities with Agamben's work on Schmitt a few years later. The conflictive protests he made his focus for five years were united by their occurrence in spaces of exceptionality, where a juridical norm or a prohibition or order laid down by the authorities has been violated (Iglesias 2008, p. 453). The supposedly pure, autonomous politics that plays out in these spaces appears in Iglesias' thesis as the only kind of politics that—through a clash between enemies that may result in death—can found true democracy. True democracy consists in the people claiming a form of sovereignty that cannot be reduced to representation in parliament. Ironically, if it were not for the lack of a strong, charismatic leader in Iglesias' account, he would have ticked all the significant boxes on a checklist for true Schmittian politics.

106 *Imagining the political future*

Evidently the tactics of the disobedients had a significant impact back at the Complutense: for their inaugural action, described earlier, members of Iglesias' and Errejón's society Contrapoder dressed up in white overalls and called for "disobedience" (Torreblanca 2015, p. 86). But as Torreblanca puts it, "something failed with the Italian *tute bianche*; even if in the eyes of Pablo Iglesias they were those who 'best understood the Zapatista strategy and tried to adapt it to advanced societies', the fact is that they failed catastrophically" (Torreblanca 2015, p. 67). This is perhaps a bit strong; the *tute bianche* and their Spanish counterparts may have failed to bring down the International Monetary Fund or the G8, but their symbolic success is more difficult to estimate. It is widely believed that the 2004 protests in front of the PP's headquarters contributed to the victory of the Partido Socialista Obrero Español (PSOE—Spanish Socialist Workers' Party) in the general elections the following day (cf. Iglesias 2008, p. 506; Hughes 2011, p. 408). Still, it is true that no regimes were toppled by the protests, and that their principal target, neoliberalism, emerged relatively unscathed. Iglesias seems disappointed that the PSOE won, because this result was "the most viable path to the [political] order's recuperation"; a PP victory would have invalidated the electoral process in the eyes of much of Spanish society, providing the perfect opportunity for "generalised strategies of disobedience" (p. 456). This attitude is a trace of a deeper conflict within Iglesias' thesis between national and post-national politics. Though he spends some time emphasising the importance of global movements that act on a post-national scale (pp. 497–502)—suggesting that parties, unions and nationalist movements that still focus on the state now suffer from "inertia"—the movements he identifies as having had the most political impact against neoliberalism are precisely those in Latin America that have sought the power of the nation-state. It is not a problem, Iglesias writes, that the movements he studied have neither desired to form nor been capable of forming governments; and yet he suggests their impact might be amplified by interacting with Latin American political projects. This is perhaps why Torreblanca suggests that Iglesias' thesis comes across "like a nut which lacks the bolt that would make it usable" (Torreblanca 2015, p. 69). The "bolt"—the portrait of the charismatic national leader with the desire and the capacity to form a government—was furnished by Juan Carlos Monedero's and Íñigo Errejón's experiences of politics under Hugo Chávez in Venezuela and Evo Morales in Bolivia respectively.

Monedero was, until his resignation in April 2015, Podemos' "number 3" and the closest among its leaders to Chávez. He too is a professor of political science at the Complutense—in fact he was part of the conference at which Llamazares was presented with the bullet and helmet—and spent some time as an advisor to Chávez' Venezuelan government between 2000

Imagining the political future 107

and 2005. In one television broadcast Chávez even referred to Monedero as "brother" and "maestro". From the outset, Torreblanca tells us, Chávez inspired Podemos' political strategy for two important reasons. First, his "personal hyperleaderism": Chávez possessed a charisma so powerful that he was able not only to stage an unsuccessful coup and end it in a televised statement of barely one minute, but, once released from prison in 1995, to be received not as the orchestrator of an illegal coup, but as a legitimate and popular political leader (Torreblanca 2015, p. 71). Secondly, Chávez had subsequently succeeded in building a movement that did not operate within the confines of either the left/right or the capitalist/anti-capitalist axes, which enabled him to unite a broad coalition of voters against the ravages of neoliberalism. His so-called "Bolivarianism" thus allowed him to steer a clever course between the nationalism of the right and the cosmopolitanism of the left (pp. 73–74). What was not to be admired in Chávez's approach? His dictatorial style, perhaps—and yet whenever Chávez was labelled a "dictator" by Spain's press, Podemos' future leaders consistently retorted: "how many dictators have won fourteen successive elections?" (p. 74). As Monedero put it, "thanks to Chávez now we can contest liberal political analysts' use of the term 'democracy'" (p. 74).

Errejón's thesis

But it is Errejón's doctoral thesis that reveals most clearly how Latin American politics predisposed Podemos' leaders to look favourably on a Schmittian breed of politics encompassing the possibility of violence, enmity and strong leadership. Errejón's history of Bolivian politics is filled with echoes of Spain's history as told by Pablo Iglesias. He sets the scene with a quote from anthropologist Pablo Regalsky, who describes the history of the Bolivian state as that of "permanent war ... over the management of space" (Errejón 2012, p. 364). In Errejón's retelling, the struggle for popular sovereignty in Bolivia has been a struggle against domestic elites empowered by foreign capital—with military force constantly in play. In the late nineteenth century Bolivia became politically fragmented as mineral expropriation funded by foreign investors—principally from Chile and Britain—pushed its way into a country already patterned by its indigenous communities and a system of *latifundismo* dating from colonial times. As foreign capital empowered domestic elites, an "oligarchic" and "*criollo* liberal state ... consolidated itself on the same fragmented political and economic geography" of colonial times. Such unstable foundations gave the state "permanent recourse" to the army to maintain its political power (pp. 365–6).

108 *Imagining the political future*

It was war that laid the foundation for the historical memory that, in Errejón's view, underlies the popular nationalism that swept current president Evo Morales to power. The Chaco War (1932–35), which was financed and instigated by Standard Oil, mobilised groups of indigenous people of various ethnicities, young nationalist officials, students and urban workers against a common military adversary (p. 367). Previously separated by cultural, geographical and economic differences, war now brought these groups together as part of a single "'imagined community'"—that of the Bolivian nation (p. 367). A "national-popular will" had been forged— one "that named the national community through the same act as it differentiated itself from the oligarchy that 'plundered the motherland' and handed it over to foreign capital" (p. 367). This newly-forged identity both laid the groundwork for and was consolidated by the 1952 revolution, and is now remembered as "one of the principal inheritances of the 'Revolución Nacional'" in the imaginary of Bolivian political life (p. 368).

For Errejón it was this national-popular identity, forged in opposition to an oligarchical elite allied to foreign powers, that became the basis of Bolivia's recent struggle against neoliberal hegemony. Neoliberal reforms began to be introduced from 1985 by a government led by the Movimiento Nacionalista Revolucionario, supported by the right-wing Acción Democrática Nacionalista, which was founded by the ex-dictator Hugo Banzer. In 1956 the government had acceded to the USA's demand that it re-establish the national army—which had been dissolved by militant workers in 1952—in return for substantial loans. (Errejón 2012, p. 369). By the mid-1980s, neoliberal reforms had become the price of foreign credit. And so the Bolivian Government reduced public spending and deregulated markets in return for external debt, eliminating the remainder of state investment in and protections for industry (pp. 374–7). State-run tin mines in the west of the country were closed; 30,000 tin miners lost their jobs, and the political organisation of the Bolivian workers' movement suffered as a result. Many were forced to turn to coca farming to support themselves and their families. Unemployment rose to 20% of the population and under-employment to 60% (p. 378). Adding insult to injury, the USA then pressured the Bolivian Government into undertaking a "long, costly, bloody and unpopular … war" against the popular cocaine syndicates (p. 380).

The political left was divided. Some of its leaders were "seduced" by the new intellectual course that neoliberalism had set, while others, less convinced, were unable to propose an alternative way out of the crisis (Errejón 2012, p. 379). Bolivian politics was now infused by a "neoliberal hegemony" which stretched to the point where even irreconcilable enemies united in coalitions behind neoliberal policy in the name of "democratic

Imagining the political future 109

responsibility". The entire elite, it seemed, was convinced of the inevitability of neoliberal reforms. This political consensus and the regime it gave rise to became known as *pactismo*, and would last until 2003 (pp. 380–81). From 1993, under the *Plan de Todos* (Plan for All), the government sought to convert the state into a facilitator of foreign investment, addressing social needs only insofar as it encouraged markets that might satisfy them. This involved the privatisation of state-run organisations and the opening of new minimally-regulated markets (Errejón 2012, p. 382). From 1994 the Government privatised five of the six largest public businesses, which brought the state 60% of its income (p. 383). This was supposed to reduce corruption—but in fact corruption continued through informal links between private enterprises and political elites (p. 383). Foreign capital sucked money out of the country without investing in training or technology within Bolivia, and lower wages paid by private businesses transferred the costs of poverty and unemployment to the state (p. 383). This left the Bolivian government in a position where it had to introduce sharp cuts in social spending to maintain its anti-deficit policy; it was also forced to sell more than 49% of its shares in public businesses. Bolivia was being impoverished as those at the centre of the world economy were being enriched (p. 384).

The political movements that would eventually bring an end to neoliberal hegemony in Bolivia rested, in Errejón's view, on three layers of historical memory. First was the long-term memory of anticolonial resistance. Second was the medium-term "nationalist anti-oligarchical and anti-imperialist" memory formed during the Chaco War and the subsequent 1952 Revolution. Third was the short-term memory of struggle against a neoliberal regime that was unable to provide for its people (Errejón 2012, p. 389). Once the state had lost any ability to satisfy even the most basic needs of its population, protests backed by this three-tiered memory began to channel themselves outside traditional political institutions and into the street (p. 384).

In 2000 the run of protests known as the *Ciclo Rebelde* (Rebel Cycle) began (Errejón 2012, p. 390). Invoking the memory of eighteenth-century independence leader Túpac Katari (p. 391), the *Ciclo Rebelde* gained momentum when the Bolivian government tried to marketise water, which until now had been considered a common resource (p. 389). There ensued what is referred to as the *Guerra del Agua* (Water War), followed soon after by the *Guerra del Gas* (Gas War) in 2003 (p. 395). To call these periods of protest "wars" is not entirely hyperbolic, since violence was a not uncommon occurrence; in 2003, for example, gunfire was exchanged in front of the presidential palace in La Paz between the police, who sided with the protesters, and the army (p. 392). Two years later the protests

110 *Imagining the political future*

brought about what Errejón considers to be the collapse not just of neoliberal hegemony but of the Bolivian state, "an institutional structure resting on a juridical fiction that excluded large swathes of Bolivian society" (p. 396).

After a succession of extremely short-lived governments, the Movimiento al Socialismo (MAS—Movement for Socialism), led by Evo Morales, swept to power in 2005 with 54% of the vote (Errejón 2012, p. 398). The MAS was a political coalition grown around a spine of former miners-turned-coca-farmers who had joined forces with indigenous groups in the 1990s. During the *Ciclo Rebelde* it had played a central role in articulating a discourse of "indigenous leftist nationalism", capable of splitting apart the neoliberal consensus. This discourse set national sovereignty against US interventionism. It denounced domestic elites as "anti-national", accusing them of selling the country to *los gringos* against the interests of "the people" (pp. 399–400). Unsurprisingly, when the MAS came to power a regional conflict opened up between the elites of the eastern departments—which represented more than half of the country's territory and of its GDP (p. 407)—and the Government, which was supported mostly by voters from the Andean and sub-Andean West (pp. 404–405).

In 2008 a constitution drafted by Morales' Government presented substantial advances in social rights, the possibility of state intervention in the economy, state "plurinationality" and political-administrative decentralisation (Errejón 2012, p. 404). This prompted the eastern departments to push for de facto autonomy, submitting proposals in the form of departmental Statutes of Autonomy to regional referenda, which were illegal in the eyes of the Government (pp. 406–407). Even the least radical of these statutes envisaged the central government ceding control over fiscal matters, the regulation of land ownership, natural resources and their exploitation, telecommunications and transport to the departmental governments (p. 407). Morales tried to resolve the dispute by holding referenda on the leadership of all the country's departments; but while his coalition made some gains, these were not enough to settle the matter (pp. 407–411).

A few weeks after the referenda, pro-autonomy protests broke out in the eastern city of Santa Cruz, mobilising members of a regionalist paramilitary group, the Unión Juvenil Cruceñista (Errejón 2012, p. 411). There ensued a wave of unrest across the eastern region, which saw state buildings occupied, the burning of union and NGO offices and attacks on government supporters (p. 411). The protesters chose targets representative of their political "enemies": the National Institute of Agrarian Reform, NGOs that worked with the indigenous Guaraní people and the premises of peasant unions (p. 481). A group affiliated to MAS was ambushed on its way to confront pro-autonomy protesters; 30 were killed (p. 411). Despite calls for the army to intervene on the side of the pro-autonomists, they kept

Imagining the political future 111

their distance (p. 411, p. 520). The government would later refer to this violent uprising as an attempted civico-prefectural coup (p. 76).

In Plan 3000, a district in the Eastern city of Santa Cruz, a coalition of union organisations and MAS supporters, known as the Frente de Resistencia del Plan 3000, formed to head off militants from the Unión Juvenil Cruceñista. During clashes between the coalition and the Unión—who had allegedly tried to burn the market, symbolically associated with immigrants from the Bolivian *altiplano* (High Plain), and the Pachamama community radio station—shots were fired and several people seriously injured. Plan 3000 and the violence that erupted there became invested with deep symbolic significance; here was an island of government support that held out against the regionalist-conservative opposition, even when faced with a paramilitary threat. Members of the Unión never managed to enter the district. President Morales later recognised the "heroic resistance" of Plan 3000 in various public speeches, as well as organising state events there. Errejón refers to the events as the "battle" of Plan 3000 (Errejón 2012, pp. 481–3).

Without the army's support, the anti-government protests dissipated. According to Bolivian Vice-President Álvaro García Linera, the Government had achieved nothing less than a military victory. Morales was subsequently able to negotiate a new draft Constitution with concessions to the eastern departments, paving the way for a political victory that saw the Congress approve Morales' constitutional referendum and the new Constitution enter into force in 2009 (Errejón 2012, p. 76).

The significance of Errejón's retelling

Errejón's thesis leaves the reader in little doubt that he admires the rise of MAS and Morales—and if there is any doubt remaining, this is eliminated when the extent to which Podemos was modelled on its Bolivian counterpart becomes clear. Both Errejón and Iglesias have quite explicitly applied the conceptual grid they have used to understand Latin American countries to Spain, even talking about Southern Europe's "latinamericanization" (Iglesias 2015b, p. 14). (Iglesias too knows the Bolivian story well; he has edited a book on Bolivian social movements and refers to Bolivia several times in his thesis—see Iglesias and López 2007; Iglesias 2008, p. 183). But the implicit correspondences between Errejón's retelling of Bolivian history and his and Iglesias' retelling of Spanish history are even more striking: they map almost directly onto one another.

Latin America's history as a colonised region might appear to be what sets it apart most conclusively from Spain. But when laying down the intellectual foundations for their new party, Iglesias and Errejón returned to Spain's nineteenth-century occupation by Napoleon's France, an

112   *Imagining the political future*

imperial power, to "latinamericanise" its history. Just as the USA had taken over from Spain as Bolivia's de facto coloniser in the twentieth century, Spain was now, in their view, under the thumb of a new colonial power: Germany. Germany is not of course a genuine colonial power in the usual sense, but that did not stop Iglesias from remarking that Southern European countries "don't want to be a colony of Germany" (Iglesias 2015c, 14:08). The stories of resistance to these colonial powers ran in parallel: in Spain there was armed resistance to Napoleon's armies during precisely the same period as Bolivia was struggling for its independence. And just as the MAS fought against US-backed neoliberal hegemony in twenty-first century Bolivia, so Podemos was now fighting against German-backed neoliberal policies in twenty-first century Spain. In both cases the neocolonial power was accused of having expropriated wealth, leaving the state incapable of meeting its population's basic needs. In both cases a direct link was drawn between the impoverishment of the South—Latin America and Southern Europe—and the enrichment of the North—the USA and Germany.

Just as, in Bolivia, MAS identified its domestic enemy as an "oligarchy" that colluded with the neocolonial USA to drain the country for its own benefit, so Podemos now identified its domestic enemy in exactly the same terms, accusing it of an identical crime. In his thesis Errejón had related how the Bolivian Government's privatisation programme increased rather than reduced corruption among the political elite; now Podemos would apply precisely the same analysis to Spain. He had explained how left-wing leaders in Bolivia were seduced by neoliberalism, and now Podemos would say the same about the Spanish PSOE. And the notion of "plurinationalism", which would take up a place at the heart of Podemos' political programme, is lifted straight out of Morales' 2008 Constitution.

The triple-layered memory Errejón detected beneath the MAS' politics was also reproduced in his and Iglesias' reconstruction of historical memory in Spain. In Bolivia's case, sandwiched between the long-term memory of resistance to imperial power and the short-term memory of resistance to neoliberalism is the medium-term memory whose sediments were laid down during the Chaco War of 1932–35 and consolidated in the National Revolution of 1952. It was militarisation, in Errejón's view, that allowed a "national-popular" will to form. At almost exactly the same time, Spain was battered by its Civil War, during which collective memories of "anti-fascist" resistance and republican values were laid down. For Errejón and Iglesias, these medium-term memories sat between those of resistance to Napoleon's troops in the nineteenth century and the recent 15-M protests in a three-layered structure that echoed the Bolivian example. In both cases, the Bolivian and the Spanish, it was predominantly militarised or partly-militarised activity that was supposed to

Imagining the political future 113

have provided the requisite historical memory for popular sovereignty to emerge.

It seems clear that Errejón, and perhaps Iglesias too, modelled Podemos' politics on the politics of MAS and Morales. "Podemos" was even originally the name of a Bolivian political party, albeit one on the right (though it is the name of a Venezuelan party too—see Torreblanca 2015, p. 186). But this had important consequences for how the Podemos leaders saw Spanish politics. In many ways contemporary political reality in Bolivia has been much more Schmittian than it has in Spain. The success of a national-popular movement has come at the cost of often violent battles against a political enemy. Errejón's account of what Vice-President García Linera referred to as the Government's "military victory" venerates the Frente de Resistencia del Plan 3000 just as Iglesias venerates the Madrid Defence Council. If what Errejón calls the "battle" of Plan 3000 was part of the Bolivian people's decisive armed struggle against their oligarchical enemy, then a similar struggle might also be necessary in Spain. Though "undesirable", violence constitutes "the ultimate possibility, it is part of the clash"; nor should violence be something that "one tries to avoid", as Mouffe suggests, because "that's where the intensity comes from. Passion comes from the intensity of the clash" (Errejón and Mouffe 2016, pp. 62–63). The success of Bolivia's national-popular movement also required the forceful guidance of a charismatic leader who has held power for over a decade and whose opponents have accused him of turning into a dictator. It should come as no surprise, then, to hear Errejón claim that it might not be possible to construct a general will without "an affective bond with a charismatic leader" (Errejón and Mouffe 2016, p. 109), and to hear him refer to Latin America as evidence for such a belief (Errejón and Mouffe 2016, p. 92).

There is another, more personal, reason for thinking that Errejón sought to import something of Bolivian politics back to its former colonial oppressor. In the early 2000s, a group of critical intellectuals known as Comuna became a think tank for the social movements and the subaltern groups' revolutionary movement (Errejón 2012, p. 39). Among this group was García Linera, who in the early 1990s participated in the "Ejército Guerrillero Túpac Katari" (Túpac Katari Guerrilla Army), a Maoist guerrilla organisation that waged an armed campaign to destroy critical infrastructure. García Linera spent five years in jail for his part in the campaign. During this time he studied sociology, and on his release worked as a sociology professor (pp. 40–41). This position allowed García Linera to develop a prominent media presence, which in turn gave him a platform from which to run alongside Evo Morales as MAS' vice-presidential candidate (p. 41).

Once in power, García Linera became indispensable due to his ability to negotiate with right-wing elites. He has managed to maintain his position

114   *Imagining the political future*

as an intellectual while in office, becoming—in Errejón's words—"the principal reference of left-wing political thought, and one of the continent's outstanding critical analysts" (Errejón 2012, p. 41). It does not seem too much of a stretch to conclude that Errejón admires this militant-turned-politician. When Podemos was founded Errejón took on a role in the party equivalent to García Linera's in the MAS, and led attempts to negotiate with the more conservative elements of the Spanish left, occasionally entering into tension with Iglesias as a result. He was frequently referred to as Iglesias' "number two". It is perhaps not surprising, then, that García Linera—who according to Errejón coined many of the terms in which contemporary discussion about Bolivian politics is conducted—is one of the principal sources in Errejón's doctoral thesis. Nor that Errejón was part of the committee that organised for a picture of Túpac Katari, the anti-colonial leader for whom García Linera's paramilitary group was named, to be painted over a wall in the Complutense (Errejón and Iglesias 2009).

García Linera embodies Iglesias and Errejón's belief that both violent and non-violent action have their place in politics—that although violence may be necessary, there comes a time to hang up the gloves. In Latin America, Iglesias's thesis counsels, the left and its popular movements have acknowledged the importance of elections—of playing "chess" rather than "boxing"—to gain at least some state power. But "there will be those who know little of this and who devour the madeleine of nostalgia for the times of the guerrillas". These people need a corrective to their thinking; they should "look at Dilma Rousseff [of Brazil], José Mujica [of Uruguay] and Álvaro García Linera; all three were *guerrilleros*, political boxers who had to learn to play chess to confront their adversaries" (Iglesias 2014a, p. 37).

Latin America: a model for Spain's future?

Schmitt's embrace of patriotism, his veneration of affective attachment to leaders, and his elevation of popular will above the constitution are all reflected in the recent experience of progressive Latin American politics. "The fear of the popular", Errejón remarked to Mouffe in their published discussion, "is clearly rooted in Europe. This might be due to our history of fascist experiences, leading many to think that fascism represents the totality of populist phenomena—or, worse, that they are their ultimate hidden truth". But for those like Errejón who have experience of "other latitudes", such memories are counterbalanced by knowledge of populist movements with "the opposite political character" (Errejón and Mouffe 2016, p. 92). In Latin America, the "identification of homeland and people crystallised into an affective identification in which leadership plays a role, and involving a relationship with opposing forces or existing institutions",

Imagining the political future 115

does not necessarily carry with it a "reactionary danger" (p. 92). It is because the Podemos intellectuals' sphere of political reference extends beyond Europe to Latin America that Iglesias can claim that "anti-systemic" movements—which have historically been either socialist or nationalist (or both)—have been the most progressive of all (Iglesias 2014a, pp. 50–51); "[A]lmost none of the great processes of historical transformation have articulated around the rhetorical poles of left/right", Errejón affirms (Errejón and Mouffe 2016, p. 129).

It is only the combination of Iglesias' and Errejón's political outlooks that provides the more fully Schmittian world view with which Podemos came to operate. This is a world view that sits on the cusp of non-liberal democracy, though it remains distinctly of the left. Having once seen the future in supranational social movements, Iglesias now recognises that the nation remains one of the most powerful "ideological devices" for constructing political identities (Torreblanca 2015, p. 151). He has raised himself above the "multitude" of militant protesters to become the charismatic leader of a traditional political formation: a party intent on gaining power through national institutions. Errejón, meanwhile, came to elevate enmity and violence in a space beyond the law to a more prominent role in his understanding of politics, seeing conflict as the "ultimate foundation" of political alignments (Errejón 2011, p. 9).

Together, Iglesias and Errejón constructed a personal-political narrative that connected the Republican regime of the 1930s with a future Spanish populism modelled partly on the Latin American left. If the nation, represented by Republican and populist movements, is the protagonist in this narrative, then Francoists and neoliberal elites are the antagonists. Ultimately it is not law, but force, that decides which of these two sides prevails; ignoring this fact can only result in political settlements that disadvantage the Spanish people and threaten the very foundations of democracy. Joining Spain's imagined past to its imagined future are the leaders of Podemos, who are helping to perform a drama far more exhilarating than anything that plays out within the walls of academia. Thus Iglesias and Errejón wrote themselves a personal-political narrative set in contemporary Spain that promised an adventure in which everything was at stake, just as Schmitt had in Weimar Germany a century earlier.

References

Errejón, Íñigo. 2011. "¿Qué es el análisis político? Una propuesta desde la teoría del discurso y la hegemonía". *Revista Estudiantil Latinoamericana de Ciencias Sociales.*

116   *Imagining the political future*

Errejón, Íñigo. 2012. *La lucha por la hegemonía durante el primer gobierno del MAS en Bolivia (2006–2009): un análisis discursivo*. Doctoral thesis (unpublished). Faculty of Political Sciences and Sociology, Complutense University of Madrid.

Errejón, Íñigo and Pablo Iglesias. 2009. "Lo que consiguió el acto de Evo Morales en la Universidad". *Rebelión*. 18 September. Available at www.rebelion.org/noticia.php?id=91665. Last accessed 27 February 2018.

Errejón, Íñigo and Chantal Mouffe. 2016. *Podemos: In the Name of the People*. London: Lawrence & Wishart.

Hughes, Neil. 2011. "'Young People Took to the Streets and all of a Sudden all of the Political Parties Got Old': The 15M Movement in Spain". *Social Movement Studies*, 10:4. pp. 407–413.

Iglesias, Pablo. 2008. *Multitud y acción colectiva postnacional: un estudio comparado de los desobedientes: de Italia a Madrid (2000–2005)*. Doctoral thesis (unpublished). Faculty of Political Sciences and Sociology, Complutense University of Madrid.

Iglesias, Pablo. 2014a. *Disputar la democracia: política para tiempos de crisis*. Madrid: Ediciones Akal.

Iglesias, Pablo. 2015b. "Understanding Podemos". *New Left Review* 93 (May-June). pp. 7–22.

Iglesias, Pablo. 2015c. "Discurso de Pablo Iglesias en la Puerta del Sol". Video available at www.youtube.com/watch?v=oe-bJXZ_KGk. Last accessed 18 February 2017.

Iglesias, Pablo and Jesús Espanandín López (eds.). 2007. *Bolivia en movimiento. Acción colectiva y poder político*. Barcelona: El viejo topo.

Torreblanca, José Ignacio. 2015. *Asaltar los cielos: Podemos o la política después de la crisis*. Second Edition. Barcelona: Penguin Random House.

6 Tensions within

In 2011 another protest group emerged out of the Faculty of Political Sciences at the Complutense University of Madrid, this time sporting a logo that looked like the kind of barcode attached to suitcases at an airport. This was the Plataforma Juventud Sin Futuro (the Youth Without Future Platform). Its rallying claim was that young Spanish people were being forced out of the country by the Government's economic choices: "We're not going [voluntarily]", its slogan read, "they're throwing us out" (Torreblanca 2015, p. 114). At the time Spain's youth unemployment rate was the second highest in Europe, surpassed only by Greece (p. 115). It was Juventud Sin Futuro that popularised the cry "Down with the regime!", setting itself up as a group of exiles opposed to a state that had failed to look after its own people (p. 116).

Juventud Sin Futuro played an important role in starting the 15-M protests, which resulted in the occupation of public squares across Spain—most famously Madrid's Puerta del Sol. The protesters set up their own system of government, establishing working commissions to manage the encampment along deliberatively democratic lines, but also to make policy proposals about healthcare, education and electoral reform—among other things (Rivero 2015, pp. 103–104). On 27 May 2011, the police charged on Barcelona's Plaça de Catalunya encampment; one hundred and twenty people were injured.

15-M signalled to Iglesias that it was possible to achieve significant things politically not principally through violent protest, but though the peaceful work of organisation. The protests were "the expression of a social indignation that, at any moment, could convert itself into a political and electoral alternative that would reorder the board of the political game" (Rivero 2015, p. 117). Whilst a minority of the 15-M protesters might have wanted to pursue a form of politics without delegation or representation, these were, in Errejón's view, only the most militant and activist; for the vast majority, the cry "they do not represent us" was not a rejection of

118   *Tensions within*

parliamentary political institutions but a rejection of the elites (Rivero 2015, p. 118). It was fundamentally a claim about who embodied the popular will.

The idea to "create a Spanish Syriza" first came up in a conversation between Pablo Iglesias and Miguel Urbán, a Complutense History graduate and parliamentary candidate for the Izquierda Anticapitalista, in mid-2013. The new party's first target would be the European elections the following year (Rivero 2015, p. 126). On 17 January 2014 Podemos was launched by Iglesias together with Urbán, Monedero and Errejón, among others. But even at this stage, Rivero notes, a tension between "the two different souls inside Podemos" was evident. In the days leading up to the party's launch, there were heated disputes about whether the "leftist" content of Podemos' inaugural manifesto should be toned down. In the end it was left unchanged. But as Carolina Bescansa (another of Podemos' founders and another Complutense professor) conceded in 2015, there is one "Podemos for winning [elections]" and another "Podemos for protesting" (Rivero 2015, p. 140).

Enmity within?

When asked by a TV interviewer whether he was a communist, Iglesias replied that "there are identities that no longer work; the important thing is to construct a decent country, not what I might have read" (Torreblanca 2015, p. 183). Torreblanca suggests that though Lenin is present in the background of Iglesias' political thought, this does not tell us much. Lenin, alongside Machiavelli and Sun Tzu, has been converted into a product for mass consumption as a "guru of tactics". But he nonetheless remains "a dangerous dogmatist with a disastrous and dangerously closed vision of the world" (p. 189). The same might be said of Schmitt. How much of the latter, "dangerous", Lenin—and how much of the latter Schmitt—Iglesias and Errejón represent is difficult to know at this stage. But Torreblanca sounds a warning: though Podemos promise a much-needed regeneration of democracy together with a vital commitment to address inequality, they do so with "an excessively Manichaean vision of society" that divides good from evil, the just from the corrupt, the wise from the wicked (pp. 190–191). One need not go beyond the history of Spain itself to see where this Donosian picture of humanity may lead. On the other hand, successful politicians must indulge in political theatre, and such oppositions are the stuff of drama. Optimism about Podemos' flirtation with Schmitt must rest on faith in their ability to keep some distance between performance and reality. That, surely, is the skill of their brand of politics.

Reality for Podemos' leaders is rarely as Schmittian as their performances, even if their rhetoric continued to bear unmistakable traces of the

Tensions within 119

German jurist's thought long after they first entered parliament. In October 2016, after two rounds of inconclusive elections, the PSOE decided to abstain in the congressional vote that determined whether Mariano Rajoy's PP could form a minority government. The PSOE's actions slotted neatly into Iglesias' Schmittian version of history: "Politics is deciding", he said, "and the PSOE has decided. It could have decided to form a government with us, but in the end it did the opposite: [it] handed the government to the Partido Popular" (El País 2016, p. 4). When it came to Podemos having to decide on its response, however, the Schmittian option no longer appeared possible.

A week earlier Iglesias had supported the idea of protests outside congress against Rajoy's investiture, suggesting that even some of Podemos' deputies might attend. The protests were being organised by a group called Coordinadora 25S. Coordinadora 25S emerged out of a similar convocation held in September 2012 during which confrontations with police resulted in 64 people being injured (Sanz et al. 2012). Now, confronted with "an illegitimate government of an illegitimate regime", it was through protest alone that, in the group's words, a true "republic" could be brought about (Coordinadora 25S 2016b). Coordinadora 25S had announced the initial meeting to organise the protest with a tweet featuring a picture of Lieutenant-Colonel Antonio Tejero brandishing his gun in the Congress (see Chapter 4); below it were the words "they have given us another coup d'état" (Coordinadora 25S 2016a). Errejón warned of the risks of Podemos' deputies becoming entangled with the protests; if they turned nasty, Podemos' political opponents would not hesitate to try to link the party to the violence (García de Blas 2016). In the eyes of the mainstream press at least, Podemos now found itself divided over whether to focus its efforts inside parliament—the route favoured by Errejón—or to strengthen its presence outside—apparently preferred by Iglesias (Manetto 2016). In the end Iglesias did not attend.

The PSOE's decision left Podemos' political strategy divided. Had it been able to form part of a parliamentary majority, Podemos might have set itself up as the carrier of a new, more democratic form of governance that channelled the sovereign will of the people directly into political action via a charismatic leader. It would have been able to decide on the state of exception. Had it remained outside parliament altogether, on the other hand, Podemos might have continued to play the Schmittian role of the partisan, contesting its enemies from the state's "constitutive outside". It would have been able to act in the gaps left by the law through protest within the state of exception. As it was, neither of these more Schmittian routes lay open to Iglesias and Errejón; instead, they were faced with the prospect of having to strike deals behind closed doors, of having to participate in lengthy discussions with opponents whose legitimacy they were

120 *Tensions within*

required to acknowledge, and of having to shun violence altogether—no matter how solely "symbolic" it was. The very liberal mode of conducting politics against which they had set themselves was, it seemed, being forced upon them by the electoral system they chose to accept, widening the breach between their Schmittian rhetoric and reality.

A split subsequently opened up between Iglesias and Errejón over how this predicament should be managed. True to the experiences recounted in his thesis, Iglesias favoured a route that would see Podemos continue to focus on its conflictive opposition from outside, mobilising street protests against the PP Government. "I think we have to subordinate our parliamentary work", he wrote in an open letter to Errejón, "to a wider strategy of constructing counter-power and alternative social institutions" (Iglesias 2016). He wanted to resist the transformation of Podemos' leadership into part of the elite, into "politicians"; they should remain activists (Iglesias 2017a, pp. 23–24). Errejón, shaped just as much by his experiences in Bolivia, favoured a path of negotiation and compromise within parliament: "We will not govern until Spain imagines us governing" (Errejón 2017).

In the run up to the second Podemos Citizen Assembly (party congress) in February 2017, Iglesias maintained that if he was re-elected as leader then the party would have to accept his vision of its future. But there was a problem with this all-or-nothing approach. Podemos' party structure is designed to encourage a degree of pluralism: the power of the secretary-general is offset by the power of the citizens' council, which decides the party's political direction. While Iglesias rejected the prospect of any disagreement between these two executive branches as hopelessly dysfunctional, Errejón and his supporters backed a motion to separate personalities from policies, lobbying for the decision about the party's future direction to be kept separate from the decision about its leadership. That way Iglesias could remain as leader even if members opted for Errejón's preferred programme (Errejón 2017). In response to Errejón's proposal, Iglesias laid down an ultimatum. If his preferred candidates, his "team", did not win a majority in the citizens' council, then he would resign as leader even if re-elected. Iglesias even put himself at the head of his preferred list of candidates for the citizens' council, entering into direct competition with Errejón, its incumbent leader. In the end Iglesias' brinkmanship was a success. Not only was he re-elected as secretary-general, with 89% of the vote; his team also won 37 of the 62 positions up for election in the citizens' council, giving them majority control (García de Blas 2017c). In a speech that followed the results, Errejón sounded a warning. "One force has emerged with a clear majority", he conceded, "but there is a clear mandate for plurality" (García de Blas 2017b).

In his open letter to Errejón, Iglesias had remarked that their relationship had been transformed into a *telenovela* (TV soap opera) by the

Tensions within 121

mainstream press, who since the outset had wanted to depict them as rivals (Iglesias 2016). He admitted that he was worried about the media's portrayal of "moderate Errejónismo" being the lesser evil when faced with "radical Pablismo". But the antagonism within Podemos was not just a media fabrication, even if it was damaging the party's public image. In the days leading up to Podemos' 2017 Citizen Assembly, Iglesias insinuated that Errejón's dissension was a betrayal of the people themselves. Diverting the party from the course set by his command was to get distracted by internal debates, massaging the egos of the leadership rather than ensuring that the people remained the true protagonists of Podemos' story (Iglesias 2017b). Unity rather than division was the only way to put the people first, Iglesias implied, and Errejón's counter-proposal undermined the strong leadership that unity required. Yet it was Iglesias himself who construed the choice between his and Errejón's proposals as a choice between "two leaderships", even though Errejón did not put himself forward for the role of secretary-general (García de Blas 2017a). Two years earlier, Errejón had cautioned that strong leadership, although desirable, might result in "decisionism" or "forms ... that can be detrimental to democracy, or to picking the best ideas" (Errejón and Mouffe 2016, p. 110). Now his concerns about the danger of getting carried away with a Schmittian performance had begun to look prescient. Errejón's position of "political secretary" on the party's citizen council was abolished—his title was changed to "secretary of strategic analysis and political change"—and his role as spokesperson given to Irene Montero, Iglesias' partner.

It might have looked like genuine Schmittian populist politics was set to emerge out of this struggle between two wings of the party—the Pablistas and the Errejónistas. Until the February 2017 Citizen Assembly there remained, as there always had been, a discrepancy between the fire of the Podemos intellectuals' Schmittian language and the relative calm of their concrete actions. But this might have been principally because of Errejón's moderating influence. Alberto Garzón, national co-ordinator of Izquierda Unida, had criticised the use of "empty signifiers" by what he dubbed Podemos' "postmodern faction", led by Errejón. Their strategy was "all heavily based on semiotics"; they seemed to believe that they could construct a people through discourse untethered from material reality. Even though Podemos was electorally successful, there was a risk that its leaders, convinced by their own talk that they were doing something radical, were in fact drifting into the "ideological moderation" of other mainstream parties (Manetto 2016). Perhaps Garzón was right at the time; it may be that the most significant material alterations produced by Podemos' rhetoric in the first three years of its existence occurred not in Spanish society but in the lives of its leaders. In which case, Schmitt's theory initially served

122 *Tensions within*

more as a tool of self-fashioning for Iglesias and Errejón—one that supported a more dramatic way of life—than it served as a blueprint for societal transfiguration.

But others feared that if Iglesias' and Errejón's commitment to Schmittian ideas went beyond a commitment to performing their way to political success—if they were committed at a more personal level too—then their Schmittian performance might become more than just performance (cf. Lassalle 2016). In Errejón's case the personal commitment to Schmittian self-transformation seemed minimal: though he admired politicians such as Bolivia's Álvaro García Linera, he appeared to be much more comfortable emulating the second part of García Linera's career than the first—the part that involved sitting around seminar and negotiating tables rather than engaging in guerrilla warfare. Iglesias, by contrast, appeared to have more appetite for embodying the archetypal decisionist politician of the left. His historical memory of Spain and the antifascist struggle, his experience of disobedience, his enthusiasm for cinematic drama and his dissatisfaction with academic life all suggested that to him Schmitt's theory was a catalyst for self-transformation. His attempts to move Podemos in a more Schmittian direction may have appeared to support this view.

Assessing the significance of Podemos' Schmittian rhetoric

That Iglesias' political language in particular has come so close to Schmitt's, however, should by no means lead us to think that Podemos advocates the kind of violence historically linked to Schmitt's thought. The violence Iglesias endorses in his thesis is explicitly *not*, in his words (written before his encounter with Schmitt via Agamben), "political violence"; it is violence that goes just far enough to have the intended symbolic effect. By engaging in low-level conflict and "dramatizing" their actions, protesters may even be able to prevent bloodier confrontations by channelling the public's energies towards symbolic victories. Iglesias shows how a small dose of violent conflict can amplify the effects of what Jeffrey Alexander understands as the symbolic struggle of democratic politics (Alexander 2011), yet does so precisely by stepping outside the boundaries of liberal democracy—and of the purely symbolic realm—itself. Large doses, however, are off limits. In a footnote in his thesis, Iglesias explains that "the uselessness of political violence for antagonistic practices in Europe" is nothing but "a cold statement of fact", demonstrated by the "absolute failure of the movements of the radical left that bet on armed struggle" (Iglesias 2008, p. 508). He and Errejón do not believe that a real risk of army-to-army war must lie behind any substantive politics. Podemos is after all much more a media organisation than a military one. But this has not

Tensions within 123

stopped its leaders from getting carried away with hyperbolic metaphor tinged with that nostalgia present in the ageing Carl Schmitt's eyes: for the disobedients whose politics Iglesias so admired, "the key to antagonistic practice" was the creation of "medieval battle" (p. 514). Iglesias makes this observation in a paragraph that compares the disobedients' philosophy to that of Georges Sorel, an inspiration to Schmitt who, in Schmitt's words, set "[a]gainst the liberal mercantilist image of balance ... another vision, the warlike image of a bloody, definitive, destructive battle" (1985, p. 69).

Nor should we necessarily read the sinister connotations of Schmitt's preferred sort of enmity into Iglesias and Errejón's words. Schmitt's retelling in the 1920s of the fable of the frogs and the storks carried a very different meaning to Iglesias' retelling in 2014 of the story of the mice and the cats. It is likely that anyone listening to Schmitt would have understood that in his mind the storks might well have been Jewish or, at the very least, French, identifiable by their physical characteristics, ethnic origin or language. Schmitt's enemy did not exist principally in the realm of the symbolic; its delineation was alarmingly concrete. Conversely Iglesias and Errejón have repeatedly refused to identify who counts as a member of the *casta* with any precision, on the grounds that doing so is unimportant. Indeed, it is Errejón's view that the term's "mobilising power comes precisely from its lack of definition" (Errejón and Mouffe 2016, p. 133). The Podemos leaders' war is principally a war of words, preoccupied with concrete details only insofar as they amplify these words' force. Iglesias' reference to "mice" may have a few symbolic hooks—Mariano Rajoy, or Esperanza Aguirre, the former President of Madrid—but its extension is otherwise deliberately left vague. Article 3 of Podemos' *Principios Organizativos* states that there is no room in the party for "any discrimination for reasons of nationality, origin, physical appearance, lineage, ethnic origin, language, disability, age, political or any other kind of opinion, religious beliefs, sex, sexual preferences, education, marital and family status, *economic situation or condition*" (Podemos 2016, p. 11, our italics). Podemos' own website discloses that Iglesias' 2014 pre-tax income was over €80,000 from the European Parliament and over €30,000 from media activities; his current account balance stood at over €125,000.

Podemos has, however, advocated the recovery of property that it alleges to have been appropriated by the Catholic Church "without any compensation to the state" (Unidos Podemos 2016, Article 339). Its election manifesto also promised to remove the subject of religion from all school curricula; to remove chaplaincies and religious services from all public institutions; to abolish laws making it a crime to offend religious feelings; and to abolish the Church's existing tax breaks (Article 293). "Justice and reparations" would be sought for victims of the Franco regime, which

124 *Tensions within*

would officially be condemned (Podemos 2015, p. 191). Though *la casta* is normally characterised as an ill-defined financial and political elite, this elite has been inextricably associated in the Podemos leaders' minds with Catholicism and with Francoism. It is difficult to escape the conclusion that for Iglesias at least the image of *la casta* morphs into that of the enemy the Republicans fought in the Civil War. But few of those active in politics today have direct links to the Franco regime. Aside from some prominent individuals, Iglesias' political enemy—even in its new incarnation as *la trama* (see Chapter 4)—is diffuse, its line of demarcation porous.

When Schmitt wrote about a homogeneous German people, perhaps he was indeed claiming that "the people" could now be "firmly and conclusively identified", arguing for "a kind of closure", as Jan-Werner Müller suggests that genuine populists do. Podemos, by contrast, intentionally refers to "the people" in what, according to Müller's own definition, is a non-populist manner; it is "committed to the idea of further inclusion" (Müller 2016, p. 73). Its 2016 manifesto calls for citizenship to be more easily accessible to foreign residents, and for the abolition of a law prohibiting foreigners from creating political parties (Unidos Podemos 2016, Article 309); it also promises measures to prevent racism, xenophobia and all other forms of discrimination (Article 313). Müller recommends that we respond to Schmittian populism by establishing who is and who is not a member of the polity through a process of democratic debate, "not a once-and-for-all decision based on unchangeable criteria" (Müller 2016, p. 81). But it is precisely this kind of debate that Podemos seeks to encourage through its participatory institutions. Once-and-for-all decisions are eschewed.

As well as fears about militarism and anti-pluralism, concerns about authoritarianism and hostility towards participation among the Podemos leadership also seem overblown. It is true that Iglesias has tried to shore up the party's hierarchy—that he advocates a kind of Schmittian rule by acclamation enabled by social media. Although Iglesias has identified television as the most important political medium of the age, it is because social media make it possible to gauge his supporters' mood that acclamation—the public expression of positive collective feeling—can be reckoned a substitute for more formally-organised mechanisms of participation (see Dean 2016). It is also true that Juan Carlos Monedero resigned because the leadership seemed to him to be losing touch with its participatory *Círculos* (circles), devoting its energies to TV appearances instead. But the most significant participatory elements of Podemos' party organisation remain intact. Contrary to Schmitt's condemnation of institutions that mechanically aggregate individual opinions in favour of what Müller calls "a noninstitutionalized notion of 'the people'" (Müller 2016, p. 31), Podemos continues to depend on online voting platforms to develop its policy.

Tensions within 125

Where real Schmittian populists "do not want people to participate continuously in politics" (p. 29), according to Müller, Podemos' leaders apparently do: their manifesto called for mechanisms through which budgets would be allocated through popular deliberation, for a "Popular Veto" allowing the public to oppose rules that directly affect them, and for spaces where politicians, technical experts and members of the general public would meet for discussions during the legislative process (Unidos Podemos 2016, Articles 226 & 227).

Müller is sceptical about left-wing strategies that draw selectively on Schmittian populism. He doubts that such attempts will succeed in mobilising "the people", and fears that they might end up importing the perils of genuine populism. Left-wing populism in Europe is therefore "either redundant or dangerous" (Müller 2016, p. 98). It would be odd to call Podemos "redundant": the party has already mobilised "the people" more successfully than any other new Spanish party in the last forty years; its populist rhetorical strategy has worked astonishingly well for the first stage of its ascent. Is it dangerous? So far, at least, Podemos' mobilisation of "the people" seems to have been achieved without bringing in its wake any of the concrete dangers so often associated with genuine Schmittian populism. But now that it has entered parliament and Iglesias has consolidated his power, might these dangers become real? Could Podemos help turn Spain into a "nondemocracy"?

Clearly the answer to this question depends on how "democracy" is defined, and it was precisely the definition of democracy that was at stake in Podemos' internal debates in early 2017. The fundamental disagreement was over whether to develop in the direction of a non-institutionalised version of democracy with Schmittian elements, or an institutionalised version of democracy that lies further from Schmitt's vision. The former, historically Iglesias' preferred route, is more comfortable with extra-parliamentary activism guided by strong leadership affirmed by acclamation. The latter, Errejón's preferred route, stresses the importance of institutions such as parliaments and organised mechanisms to facilitate the party membership's participation. Each route is more "populist" in a different sense: the first, because it remains hostile to parliamentary elites, the second, because it provides for continuous and genuine participation. If there is so much tension between these routes that the party falls to pieces, Podemos could still end up being "redundant". If the wrong mixture of these routes unfolds, it could steer Spain towards "nondemocracy". But surely there is also a chance that—in part because of its engagement with Schmittian populism and its incisive political critique—Podemos will be the agent of democracy's revitalisation.

References

Alexander, Jeffrey. 2011. *Performance and Power*. Cambridge: Polity.

126 *Tensions within*

Coordinadora 25S. 2016a. "Las calles no pueden estar vacias ante este #Golpe-DeEstado Convocamos a organizaciones sociales/políticas #DecisiónPsoeARV #PSOEDecideM4". *twitter.com/Coordinador25S.* 18 October, 3:32am. Available at https://twitter.com/Coordinadora25S/status/788326875886149632/photo/1?ref_src=twsrc%5Etfw. Last accessed 27 February 2018.

Coordinadora 25S. 2016b. "Ante el Golpe de la Mafia, Democracia". *coordinadora25s.wordpress.com.* 25 October. Available at https://coordinadora25s.wordpress.com/2016/10/25/ante-el-golpe-de-la-mafia-democracia/. Last accessed 27 February 2018.

Dean, Mitchell. 2016. "Political acclamation, social media and the public mood". *European Journal of Social Theory.* April. pp. 1–18.

El País. 2016. "Así ha sido la ronda de consultas previa a la investidura de Mariano Rajoy". *politica.elpais.com.* 25 October. Available at https://politica.elpais.com/politica/2016/10/25/actualidad/1477379883_381550.html. Last accessed 27 February 2018.

Errejón, Íñigo. 2017. "Recuperar la iniciativa". *información.es.* 5 February. Available at www.diarioinformacion.com/opinion/2017/02/05/recuperar-iniciativa/1857108.html. Last accessed 27 February 2018.

Errejón, Íñigo and Chantal Mouffe. 2016. *Podemos: In the Name of the People.* London: Lawrence & Wishart.

García de Blas, Elsa. 2016. "El manifiesto de la convocatoria de Rodea el Congreso cuestiona el régimen democrático". *El País.* 28 October. Available at http://politica.elpais.com/politica/2016/10/28/actualidad/1477646516_793509.html. Last accessed 27 February 2018.

García de Blas, Elsa. 2017a. "Iglesias convierte la pugna con Errejón en un plebiscito sobre su liderazgo". *El País.* 3 February. Available at http://politica.elpais.com/politica/2017/02/02/actualidad/1486023564_361518.html. Last accessed 27 February 2018.

García de Blas, Elsa. 2017b. "Errejón no da un paso atrás y pide a Iglesias respetar el mandato de pluralidad". 12 February. Available at http://politica.elpais.com/politica/2017/02/12/actualidad/1486890767_251692.html. Last accessed 27 February 2018.

García de Blas, Elsa. 2017c. "Iglesias logra todo el control para imponer el Podemos más radical". 13 February. Available at http://politica.elpais.com/politica/2017/02/12/actualidad/1486890748_595172.html. Last accessed 27 February 2018.

Iglesias, Pablo. 2008. *Multitud y acción colectiva postnacional: un estudio comparado de los desobedientes: de Italia a Madrid (2000–2005).* Doctoral thesis (unpublished). Faculty of Political Sciences and Sociology, Complutense University of Madrid.

Iglesias, Pablo. 2016. "Carta abierta a Íñigo". *20 Minutos.* 12 December. Available at www.20minutos.es/opiniones/pablo-iglesias-carta-abierta-inigo-2909440/#xtor=AD-15&xts=467263. Last accessed 27 February 2018.

Iglesias, Pablo. 2017a. *Plan 2020: ganar al Partido Popular gobernar España*. Available at https://pabloiglesias.org/wp-content/uploads/2017/01/Plan_2020_def.pdf. Last accessed 27 February 2018.

Iglesias, Pablo. 2017b. "Podemos: la película". *lamarea.com*. 6 February. Available at www.lamarea.com/2017/02/06/podemos-la-pelicula/. Last accessed 27 February 2018.

Lassalle, José María. 2016. "Gran coalición o empate catastrófico". *El País*. 14 July.

Manetto, Francesco. 2016. "La manifestación que llama a rodear el Congreso divide a Podemos". *El País*. 26 October. Available at http://politica.elpais.com/politica/2016/10/25/actualidad/1477382980_781970.html. Last accessed 27 February 2018.

Müller, Jan-Werner. 2003. *A Dangerous Mind: Carl Schmitt in Post-War European Thought*. New Haven, CT: Yale University Press.

Müller, Jan-Werner. 2016. *What is Populism?*. Philadelphia: University of Pennsylvania Press.

Podemos. 2015. *Podemos 26J*. Available at https://lasonrisadeunpais.es/wp-content/uploads/2016/06/Podemos-Programa-Electoral-Elecciones-Generales-26J.pdf. Last accessed 27 February 2018.

Podemos. 2016. *Principios Organizativos*. Available at https://podemos.info/wp-content/uploads/2016/11/Principios_organizativos_castellano.pdf. Last accessed 27 February 2018.

Rivero, Jacobo. 2015. *Podemos. Objetivo: asaltar los cielos*. Barcelona: Editorial Planeta.

Sanz, L. A., J. Manso, X. Méndez, Á. Carvajal. 2012. "Cargas, 35 detenidos y 64 heridos". *El Mundo*, 26 September. Available at www.elmundo.es/elmundo/2012/09/24/espana/1348502415.html. Last accessed 27 February 2018.

Schmitt, Carl. 1985. *The Crisis of Parliamentary Democracy*. Translated by Ellen Kennedy. London: The MIT Press.

Torreblanca, José Ignacio. 2015. *Asaltar los cielos: Podemos o la política después de la crisis*. Second Edition. Barcelona: Penguin Random House.

Unidos Podemos. 2016. *Programa*. Available at https://lasonrisadeunpais.es/programa/. Last accessed 27 February 2018.

Index

15-M movement 8–9, 11–13, 33, 117–18
23-F coup attempt *see* coup attempt of February 1981

acclamation 25–7, 52, 124–5
Agamben, Giorgio 38–40, 92, 105, 122
agonism (versus antagonism) *see* antagonism
Amnesty Law of 1977 2, 71
antagonism (versus agonism) 36–8
Asociación para la Recuperación de la Memoria Histórica (Association for the Recovery of Historical Memory, ARMH) 76–8
austerity policies 58–9, 83–4; in Bolivia 109

Basque Country 35, 54, 80–3
Bavarian Soviet Republic of 1919 48–9
Benjamin, Walter 38–40
Bolivia 107–14

casta 10, 33, 88; definition of 123; displacement by *trama* 91–2
Catalonia 35, 54
Catholic Church / Catholicism 29, 123–4
Chávez, Hugo 69, 106–7
Ciudadanos 10
Civil War, Spanish 28, 70–4; accuracy of statistics about 74, 77; Podemos leaders' views of 84–5, 94–5
collective will 32, 58

Conde, Francisco Javier 29–30, 93
Constitution: of contemporary Spain 55–6, 59–60, 72, 87, 90; of the German Empire 47; of the Weimar Republic 50, 52–3
Contrapoder 69, 106
corruption 10, 86, 89, 109, 112
coup attempt of February 1981 72–3, 86, 104

decisionism 22, 35, 67, 88, 122
democracy: definition of 25–7, 105, 125; direct 52; deliberative 125
dictatorship 27, 35, 107; Schmitt's view of 50–1
desobedientes (disobedients) 103–4, 123
Donoso Cortés, Juan 1, 30, 51, 65–7

economicism in politics 58–60
emotion in politics 32, 58, 96
Errejón, Íñigo:
  early life 68
  at the Complutense 68–70, 106–7
  in Bolivia 107
European Union (EU) 9, 16, 56–8, 72, 80
Euskadi Ta Askatasuna (ETA) 40, 54, 68, 80–3, 92; blamed for 2004 Madrid bombings 86 105

Fascism
financial crisis of 2008 56, 83, 88–9, 91
Fraga, Manuel 81, 93
Franco, Francisco 29, 71–2

Index 129

franquismo (Francoism) 11, 80, 93, 124
friend/enemy distinction 23–4, 37–8, 87–8, 123

García Linera, Álvaro 111, 113–14, 122
Garzón, Baltasar 10, 75, 82
Germany: during the Weimar Republic *see* Weimar Republic; power within the European Union 9–10, 34, 56–8, 83, 112
González, Felipe 59, 75, 83, 91
Gramsci, Antonio 9, 12, 15, 34, 36, 40

Hardt, Michael 41
hegemony 12, 108–10
homogeneity: in Schmitt's political theory 23, 26–7, 51–2, 54, 124
Hitler, Adolf 20, 46, 51, 53–4, 83

indignadossee 15-M movement
Iglesias, Pablo: early life 68; at the Complutense 68–70; in Italy 101–3
individualism 24, 60
inequality 11, 26–7, 32–3, 58
Instituto de Estudios Políticos 30, 93, 41n1
Izquierda Unida (IU) 8, 17, 104–5, 121
Italy 51, 101–3

Juventud Sin Futuro (Youth Without Future) 117–18

Laclau, Ernesto 9, 12, 15
Lassalle, José María 60–1, 86, 88–9, 91
Latin America 35–6, 107–14; connections with Podemos 69, 106–7; independence from Spain 66; *latinamericanization* of Southern Europe 13, 111; as model for Spain 114–15
Law of Historical Memory (2007) 77
left/right distinction in politics 4, 13–15, 37–8, 115
Legaz Lacambra, Luis 30, 81, 93
liberalism 24–5, 31–2, 56, 60, 66–7, 91
Linz, Juan 60–1, 90–1

Madrid Defence Council (1936–7) 84, 94
Maravall, José María 59–60, 86–8, 91
Marxism 2, 9, 12, 55
Monedero, Juan Carlos 69–70, 106–7, 118, 124
Morales, Evo 69, 108, 110–13
Mouffe, Chantal 12, 15, 36–8
Mussolini, Benito 51, 96
myth in politics 27, 32, 51, 96, 102

Napoleon Bonaparte 83; 1808–14 occupation of Spain 28 33–5, 65–6, 112
narrative structure 5–6, 61–2, 65, 115
National Socialist German Workers' (Nazi) party 20, 46, 51–3, 55; Schmitt's association with *see* Schmitt, Carl
Negri, Antonio 41
neoconservatism 88–9
neoliberalism 31–2, 60, 95–6, 102, 106–7, 112; in Bolivia 108–10

oligarchy 11, 91–2, 112; in Bolivia 107–9, 112

Pact of Forgetting 71–7, 85
parliamentarism 24–6, 52, 56
Partido Popular (PP): corruption in 10; foundation of 75, 81, 93; policies of 58–9, 75, 77, 86–7, 105
Partido Socialista Obrero Español (PSOE): 2004 election victory 106; 2016 election negotiations 119; policies of 8, 56–8, 76–7, 79–80, 84, 90–1; armed campaign against ETA 81–3
partisan: Schmitt's theory of 28–9, 33–4
performance 6, 96, 118–19, 122
performativity 93
Pinochet, Augusto: arrest of 75–6
pluralism 36, 53 120
plurinationality 69, 110, 112
Podemos: 2014 EU elections 16; 2015 elections 16; 2016 elections 17, 57, 124; change in stance of 91–2; foundation of 9, 118; internal tension within 118–22, 125; party structure of 15–16, 124; pluralism

130 *Index*

within 120–124; Second Citizen Assembly of (2017) 120–22
political: autonomy of the 13, 21, 105; definition of the 23–4
populism: nature of 6–7, 124–5; in contemporary politics 88–9, 124–5; in Latin America 114–15
positioning, intellectual 4

Rajoy, Mariano 10, 17, 54, 59, 77, 87, 119, 123
Reig Tapia, Alberto 89–90
Rodríguez Zapatero, José Luis 10, 56, 76–7, 84, 87
referendum 52, 111
Republic, First Spanish (1873–4) 71, 85
Republic, Second Spanish (1931–6) 30, 33, 56, 71, 80, 84

Schmitt, Carl: association with the National Socialist Workers' Party (Nazis) 20, 46, 51–3; development of ideas 46; in Berlin 20; in Munich 50–1; in Spain 1–2, 28–9; influence of Donoso Cortés on 1, 51, 67; vision of politics 21–31
Sorel, Georges 27, 123
social democracy 10, 87, 91
sovereignty 9, 23, 35, 66, 110
state of exception 21–23, 38–40, 80–2, 86; in spaces of exceptionality 102

Tejero, Lieutenant-General Antonio 73, 104, 119
television in politics 9, 14–15, 70, 124
Transition (1978) 11, 78–80, 89–90
trama see casta
Troika 33, 56–8, 83
Tronti, Mario 2–3
tute bianche 102–3

Universidad Complutense de Madrid (Complutense University of Madrid) 8, 68–70, 86, 117–18

Venezuela 13, 69, 106, 113

Weimar Republic 8, 30, 46–62